Table of Contents

Table of Contents	2
Introduction	6
About	7
When to Enjoy Dessert	8
Sugar is Harmful to your Health	9
Sugar Alternatives	10
Honey	10
Maple Syrup	10
Stevia	11
Coconut Sugar	11
Other Sweeteners	12
Baking Substitutes	13
Eggs	13
Butter	13
Milk	14
Chocolate	15
Flour	16
Conversions	17
Imperial to Metric Conversion	17
Measurement Equivalents	17
Guest Authors	18
Andrea Kmecza	18
Lynsey Franklin	18
Alexis Nilsen	19
Meha Sethi	19
Mandy King	20
Sarah Bester	20
Deanna Harris	21
Andra Trambitas	21
Devina Daya	22
Deiala Abdallah	22
Acknowledgements	23

Want More?	88
Holistic in the City	89
7 Days of Smoothies	90
21 Day Smoothie Guide	91
Affiliate application	92
Let's get Social	93

Recipes

Recipe Information	25
Raw Blueberry Cheesecake	27
Raw Lemon Cheesecake Tarts	29
Raw Mojito Squares	31
Chocolate Avocado Pudding	33
Black Forest Brownies	35
Healthy Pea(not) Butter Cups	37
Almond Carob Tarts	39
Homemade Chocolate Bar	41
Carob Hazelnut Bark	43
Dark Chocolate Chili Bites	45
Quinoa Cocoa Cupcakes	47
Carob Cake with Fudge Icing	49
You wish Tim Horton's Donuts	51
Chocolate Basil Cake	53
Almond Coconut Choco Chip Cookies	55
Gluten Free Blueberry Cookies	57
Real Food Gingerbread	59
Lemon Oatmeal Cookies	61
Oatmeal Cookie Truffles	63
Chocolate Hazelnut Truffles	65
Superfood Choco Truffles	67
Protein Power Balls	69
Date Bliss Balls	71
Pine Nut Tart	73
Upside Down Pear-Banana Cake	75
Carrot Cake Cupcakes	77
Pear Apple Pie Crumble	79
Strawberry Rhubarb Crisp	81
Vegan Blueberry Ice Cream	83
Banana Protein "Ice Cream"	85
Peanut Butter Soft Serve	87

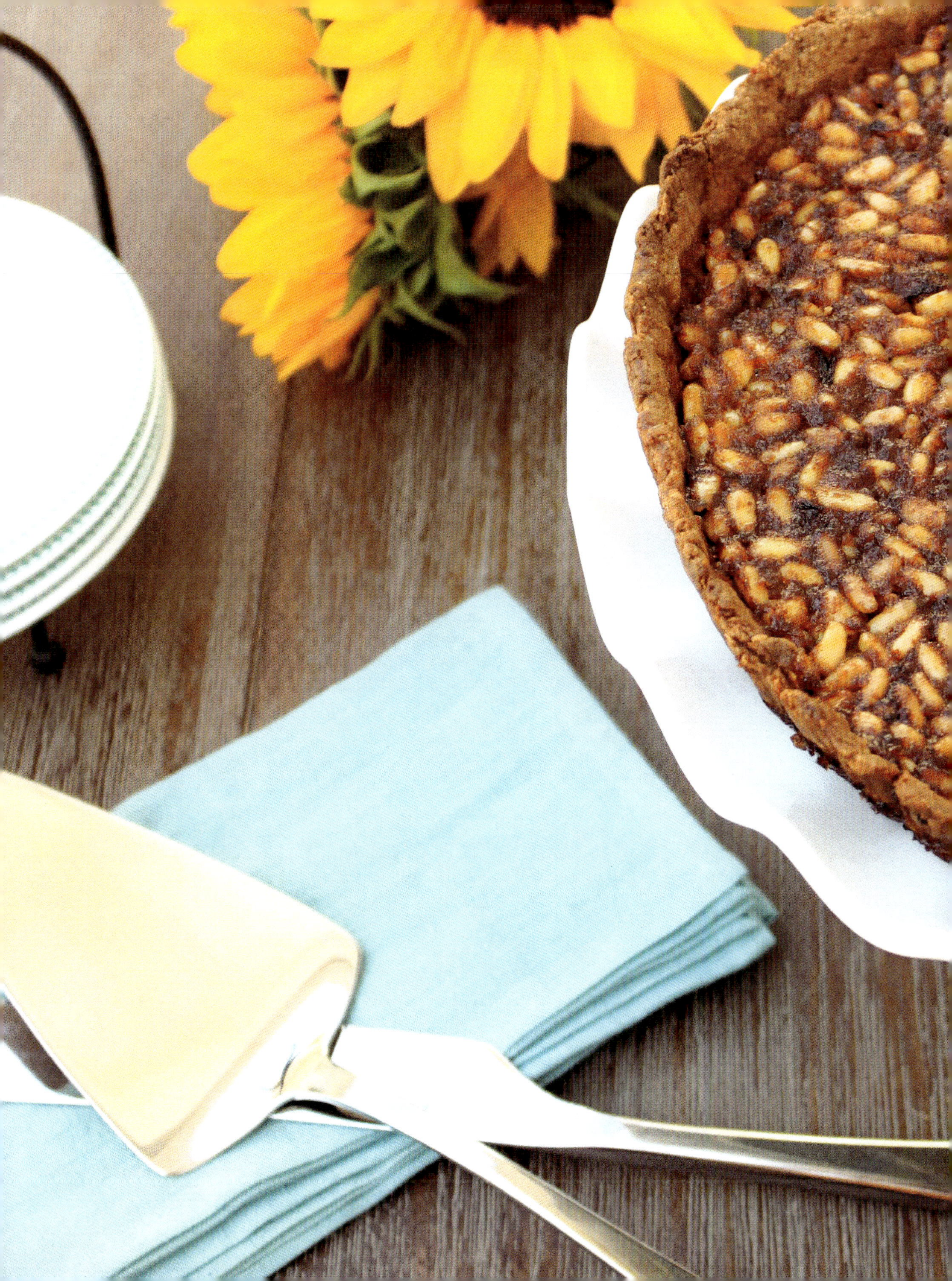

Introduction

Hello, my name is Jesse Lane and I'm a sugar-a-holic.

Being a sugar fiend runs in my family and I am no exception. Whenever we slept over at our Bubby's (Jewish Grandmother), she would offer us dessert at every meal and EVERYONE would eat it, even if it was 8 am.

When I was growing up, we had an exchange student from Japan live with us for several years.

He was astounded by the amount of sugar, dessert and candy my sisters and I consumed and coined us "sugar busters".

I was fortunate to grow up with a Mom who is an incredible cook who made us delicious and healthy meals. Since my sisters and I were so into desserts, she taught us how to bake at an early age. This was fantastic because most of the sweets we consumed were homemade and free from preservatives, chemicals and everything else you find in store bought goods. I have two sisters and with everyone baking, there were always plenty of sweets in the house.

For the longest time sugar didn't bother me, but eventually I started experiencing Candida symptoms. Candida is a yeast organism that can flourish in different parts of the body and feeds on sugar. After learning more about Candida, I knew I had to make a change.

I began by decreasing the amount of sugar I was eating and did a Candida cleanse. After I was certain that the yeasty-beasties were under control, I started eating homemade sweets again that were made with alternative sweeteners.

I had so much fun creating recipes that I started writing them down. I'm so excited to share those recipes with you today!

This cookbook contains lots of my recipes along with recipes sent to me by other fantastic Holistic Nutritionists. All of the recipes are made with whole food ingredients and do not contain any soy, dairy, white flour or processed sugar. Most of the ingredients are also super easy to find as well.

www.jesselanewellness.com

About

I'm Jesse Lane Lee, BSc, CNP, and I am a cheerful Holistic Nutritionist, motivating speaker, cookbook author and wellness writer. I am the founder of JesseLaneWellness.com, a web based holistic nutrition practice and holistic recipe resource.

I have struggled with Irritable Bowel Syndrome and food allergies on and off for most of my life, starting when I was a baby! I knew something had to change when the Irritable Bowel Syndrome symptoms I was experiencing kicked into high gear while I was studying Engineering at University. I was getting sick so often that I was constantly anxious and worrying about where the washroom was in every building or situation I found myself in.

I started my healing journey by visiting a holistic practitioner who gave me the guidance I needed to heal my leaky gut. As I gathered momentum, I became really excited about cooking healthy food and I started to play in the kitchen.

I had so much fun creating allergen free recipes and the restrictive diet I was following became a source of culinary inspiration.

Today, I feel fantastic and am able to enjoy most of the foods that used to cause an unwelcome reaction.

I love to experiment in the kitchen and create holistically delicious recipes that accommodate a wide variety of food allergies, diets and lifestyle choices. I am a co-author of The Holistic In the City 21 Day Smoothie Guide which contains 21 delicious smoothie recipes made with love by 7 Holistic Nutritionists. I am also a regular recipe contributor to KrisCarr.com, OneGreenPlanet.org and MindBodyGreen.com.

I believe that eating healthy whole foods can be easy, fun and most of all delicious!

When to Enjoy Dessert

When I was a kid the rule was you couldn't have dessert until you finished everything on your plate. Since I was such a "sugar buster", this was motivation for me to finish all the trees (aka broccoli) on my plate. I was also really smart and ALWAYS left room for dessert.

What my parents didn't know is that it is actually better to enjoy dessert before dinner or as a snack!

Dessert tends to be high in sugar and simple carbohydrates so it digests really quickly. When you eat dessert right after dinner, it sits on top of the more slowly digesting dinner foods, breaks down and starts to ferment. The fermentation of digested sugars leads the unpleasant bloating and gas.

The best time to eat dessert is 30 minutes before a meal or 3 hours after.

Sugar is Harmful to your Health

The average adult consumes their own body weight in sugar.

Think about how much that is!

Sugar is completely void of protein, fiber, vitamins, minerals, healthy fats and enzymes. In fact, its lack of nutrients creates an acidic environment. When you eat sugar your body has to actually pull nutrients from its store to correct this imbalance.

This makes sugar an anti-nutrient.

Sugar is also very highly addictive. It is often compared to cocaine and can be just as habit-forming as any narcotic. You truly can be addicted to sugar!

Is there a solution?

Kinda.

In an ideal world we would get all of our sugar from natural sources that are not refined, basically from whole fruit.

BUT if you love dessert as much as I do, this simply isn't practical.

I recommend eating homemade desserts in moderation and using sweeteners that contain nutrients like the ones mentioned this book.

I also recommend enjoying desserts that are high in fiber because it slows down the release of sugar into the blood stream. This helps avoid a sugar high which is inevitably followed by a crash.

Here are my top four sweeteners.

Sugar Alternatives

Maple Syrup

I'm from Canada where maple syrup is super popular and very reasonably priced. It is made by boring holes (or tapping) maple trees, collecting the sap and boiling it for an extended period of time to concentrate the syrup. My dad actually tapped his trees one year and the syrup he made was the best I have ever tasted.

I like using maple syrup because it contains antioxidants and minerals like manganese, zinc, calcium, iron, magnesium and potassium.

When buying maple syrup make sure you are buying a product that contains pure maple syrup, not maple flavored corn syrup. Real maple syrup comes in two grades, grade A which ranges from light amber to dark amber and grade B which is super dark. The main difference is that the darker syrups have a stronger maple flavor. You can use whichever kind you like for the recipes in this cookbook.

Honey

Did you know honey is pretty much bee vomit? It is flower pollen extract that is digested and regurgitated by bees! It sounds gross but it is actually super clean. In fact, honey is antibacterial, antimicrobial and antiseptic.

While honey is high in fructose, it has many health benefits and contains B vitamins, vitamin C, D and E.

Similar to maple syrup not all honey is created equal. When buying honey make sure you read the label, or better yet talk to the farmer who made it, to make sure it is raw, unfiltered and 100% pure honey.

Stevia

I love using Stevia as a sweetener in my desserts.

Stevia is a super sweet zero calorie herb that does not affect your blood sugar or insulin secretions.

In fact, studies have shown that stevia actually improves cellular insulin sensitivity which lowers the risk of diabetes and high blood pressure.

Taste wise stevia is super sweet with a bitter undertone; 1 tsp of stevia is equivalent to 1 cup of sugar in sweetness.

When you are buying stevia it is really important to look for a green powdered stevia which has been made by simply dehydrating stevia leaves.

Stevia gets a bad rap because there are tons of brands that contain fillers so it can be substituted one for one with sugar.

Coconut Sugar

Coconut sugar has a glycemic index of 35 which is pretty low for a sweetener considering regular table sugar has a glycemic index of 65.

Glycemic index is a number that ranges from 0-100 that tells you how different foods affect your blood sugar and insulin production. The lower the glycemic index, the less it affects blood sugar and insulin levels.

Coconut sugar is made from the sap and nectar of coconut palm trees.

I like using coconut sugar because it can be substituted one-for-one with regular sugar. It is most similar to brown sugar so it will add a slight caramel like flavor to your baking.

Other Sweeteners

You will also see other sweeteners in this cookbook like;

Apple Sauce			Packed with fiber! Be sure to buy unsweetened and unflavored.

Bananas			Make sure they are nice an brown for extra sweetness

Medjool Dates		Another fiber packed sweetener.

Blackstrap molasses	Blackstrap molasses is less processed and lower glycemic index than fancy molasses. It also retains the nutrients stripped from sugar cane so it is really high in iron and other minerals.

Baking Substitutes

Eggs

Eggs are a very common allergen which can be found in the majority of baked goods and other packaged products. Non-organic eggs contain hormones and antibiotics which adversely affect our health and wellbeing. Eggs are an excellent source of protein, so if you don't have a problem digesting eggs I suggest you buy organic eggs to avoid the hormones and antibiotics.

For those sensitive to eggs or following a vegan diet, you can use a flax or chia egg.

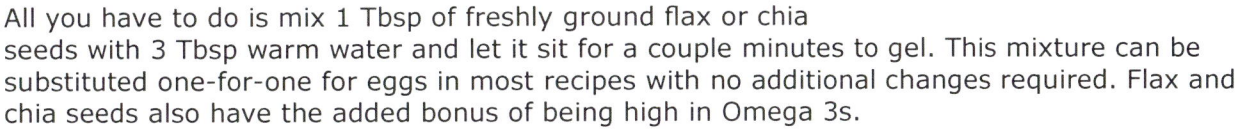

All you have to do is mix 1 Tbsp of freshly ground flax or chia seeds with 3 Tbsp warm water and let it sit for a couple minutes to gel. This mixture can be substituted one-for-one for eggs in most recipes with no additional changes required. Flax and chia seeds also have the added bonus of being high in Omega 3s.

Butter

I love Butter. I was known to eat it with my fingers when I was a kid! When shopping for butter I strongly recommend buying organic butter, or better yet, organic butter from grass fed cows. Similar to milk, conventional butter contains hormones, growth factor and antibiotics.

If you follow a vegan diet, coconut oil makes a fantastic butter substitute.

It is true that coconut oil is mostly saturated fat, but not all saturated fats are created equal. Coconut oil is made up of medium chain triglycerides that your body converts immediately into energy and does not store as fat. It has also been proven to lower cholesterol levels!

When buying coconut oil look for a product that is virgin, cold pressed and stored in a glass container. Coconut oil can be substituted one-for-one with butter in most recipes.

Share your creations with #JLWCookbook

Milk

Human babies are intended to drink breast milk for the first few years of life, not cow's milk.

The composition of cow's milk is actually quite different from breast milk. It contains much more sodium, protein and calcium and no vitamin C.

Non organic milk contains hormones, growth factor and antibiotics.

After babies are weaned, it is very common for them to lose the ability to create the enzymes necessary to properly digest dairy. This is why a lot of people are lactose intolerant.

Consuming dairy when you can't properly digest it can lead to:

Digestive distress	bloating, gas, abdominal cramps, constipation, diarrhea
Skin conditions	acne, hives, rashes
Pain	joint, arthritic, headaches

Stuffy nose

Personally, I believe that dairy does not have to be part of a complete diet; there are plenty of plant based sources of calcium like sesame seeds, collard greens and spinach.

In this cookbook you will see recipes calling for almond milk or any milk alternative (rice, hemp, coconut ...).

Nut milks can also be easily substituted one-for-one with regular milk.

Chocolate

Chocolate contains caffeine and is a common allergen (I'm actually sensitive to it!) so it's not suitable for everyone. Don't get me wrong, I love my chocolate and there are tons of chocolate recipes in the cookbook, but it's fun to mix it up every now and then.

Carob is a legume that comes from a tree native to the Mediterranean, the seed pods are commonly ground to make a sweet dark powder that has caramel and earthy undertones.

Carob is naturally caffeine free and is high in antioxidants that help prevent free radical damage and signs of aging.

Compared to chocolate, carob is three times richer in calcium and it contains high amounts of fibre. In fact, the fibre found in carob absorbs liquid and has a binding action in the intestinal tract that can help relieve digestive problems like diarrhea.

Carob tastes a little different than chocolate, but it can be substituted one-for-one in any recipe.

There are some recipes in the cookbook that call for chocolate chips or dark chocolate. If you are sensitive to chocolate you can use carob chips which are found in most health food stores. If you have a dairy allergy, make sure you read the label of the chocolate you are buying, there are lots of brands that make dairy free chocolate chips and dark chocolate bars.

Alternatively you can use the dairy free "Homemade Chocolate Bar" (page 41) and cut it into chocolate chunks.

Flour

Gluten is a sticky grain protein found in wheat, rye and barley. It sticks to the cilia in your intestines making it difficult for your body to absorb essential vitamins and nutrients.

Not everyone is sensitive to gluten; however, refined white flour offers very little nutritional value.

Excellent gluten free flours used in this cookbook include:

- Almond flour
- Coconut flour
- Brown rice flour
- Quinoa flour

All of these flours are commonly found in grocery stores all ready to go.

Alternatively, you can make your own by grinding whole grains or nuts in a high powered blender, a coffee grinder (in very small batches!) or a grain mill.

I also love using spelt flour in my recipes. It is not gluten free but spelt is an ancient grain that is easier to digest than regular white or whole wheat flour.

Spelt four contains more protein and vitamin B2 than whole wheat flour and gives baking a yummy nutty flavor.

Gluten free flours and spelt flour cannot be substituted one-for-one for regular or whole wheat flour. When using spelt flour, substitute 1.5 cups of spelt flour for every 1 cup of flour.

Conversions

Imperial to Metric Conversion

Imperial	Metric
1/5 tsp	1 ml
1 sp	5 ml
1 Tbsp	15 ml
1 fluid oz.	30 ml
1/5 cup	50 ml
1 cup	240 ml
2 cups (1 pint)	470 ml
4 cups (1 quart)	950 ml (0.95 litre)
4 quarts (1 gal)	3.8 litres
1 oz.	28 grams
1 pound	454 grams

Measurement Equivalents

Measurement	Equivalent
1/16 tsp	dash
1/8 tsp	a pinch
3 tsp	1 Tbsp
1/8 cup	2 Tbsp
1/4 cup	4 Tbsp
1/3 cup	5 Tbsp + 1 tsp
1/2 cup	8 Tbsp
3/4 cup	12 Tbsp
1 cup	16 Tbsp
1 lb	16 oz

Guest Authors

Andrea Kmecza is a Certified Nutritional Practitioner (CNP) and is the creator of Delectably Simple, a blog dedicated to recipe creating, sharing and food photography. Gastropost regularly features her food photos in the National Post newspaper.

During her career in the airline industry, Andrea pursued her passion for food and holistic health by earning her diploma in Applied Holistic Nutrition from the Institute of Holistic Nutrition. She is passionate about helping others achieve optimal health and wellness through conscious eating and lifestyle choices.

Her travelling inspired her to develop and create a number of recipes. She loves creating healthy new recipes, and giving traditional ones "makeovers". Her goal is to create recipes that are easy to make, delicious and most of all healthy. Cooking should be fun and simple!

Find her at her website: www.DelectablySimple.blogspot.ca.

Lynsey Franklin is a Holistic Nutritionist (CNP), Certified Personal Trainer, Health coach and Owner/Founder of Elevate Fitness and Nutrition, based in Guelph.

Lynsey is passionate about helping you to become the best YOU yet. She wants to help you become healthier and feel and look your absolute best, by eating healthy with real food, making lifestyle changes and supplementation if needed. She enjoys finding ways of making exercise fun in a gym atmosphere or at home! She is 100 percent committed to helping you take your health and fitness to the next level. She will customize a plan that is specific to your individual needs and goals, while addressing the root cause and focusing on prevention.

Lynsey is very excited to inspire and empower you as you embark on your journey towards optimal health and the best you yet!

Connect with Lyndsay on
Instagram: @elevatefitnessandnutrition or @ lynseydf_cnp;
send her an email at elevatefitnessandnutrition@yahoo.com.

Alexis Nilsen is a holistic nutritionist and writer for Clean Eating Magazine. She makes gluten and dairy free look good. Some would call Alexis the poster child of health; Quinoa, Kale and Avocado are just a few of her favorite words. She loves grocery shopping more than shoe shopping, and if you can't find her in the kitchen it's probably because she is in the middle of a downward dog or one mile in on a nature hike.

Connect with Alexis at her website: www.CowCrumbs.com
or on Instagram: @cowcrumbs

Meha Sethi is a holistic nutritionist with a background in Marketing and Trade. Meha Sethi believes that to be truly healthy and vibrant we must go beyond just the foods we eat but also focus on using only the cleanest and purest products on our skin. She is currently in the process of creating an online boutique for woman who want to feel and look their best while knowing that the products they are choosing are safe, luxurious, sustainable and cruelty-free.

Connect with her on Instagram: @ms.wellness

Mandy King is a Holistic Nutritionist and the founder of HEAL. She works with health conscious women who want to take control of their health to stop feeling tired, fix their digestion and lose the weight once and for all. She helps them create a lasting, lifestyle change that not only helps them look good in their skinny jeans, but feel good and have the energy to do whatever they want so they can worry less and have more time and confidence for what matters.

Find Mandy at her website: www.HealthyEatingAndLiving.ca
Instagram: @HealthyEatingAndLiving_ca
Facebook: @HealthyEatingAndLiving.ca
Twitter: @HealthyEatingAndLiving.ca

Sarah Bester is a Family Nutritionist and Real Food Educator. She helps kids (and families) develop a healthy relationship with real food in order to support a long and absolutely vibrant life. Sarah's goal is to prove to you that your kids CAN learn to love and appreciate vegetables (or even just tolerate them!) and that it can be fun instead of a battle.

Connected with Sarah at her website: www.SarahBester.com
Instagram: @KidsHeartRealFood
Facebook: @KidsHeartRealFood

Deanna Harris is a Holistic Nutritionist and recipe/wellness blogger passionate about fresh foods, farmers markets and home cooking. She loves exposing people to the nature of holistic living by sharing delicious recipes & health videos. Deanna is the author of Baking Gluten-free and Vegan: 10 Allergy Friendly Desserts e-book and the voice behind Nature's Peach. She is a REAL food advocate with a passion for deliciously nutritious recipes. Deanna loves to keep things SIMPLE, FRESH and WHOLESOME.

Visit her blog at www.naturespeach.com
Instagram: @naturespeach

Andra Trambitas, CNP is a Holistic Nutritionist and yoga teacher. She foundered Blossoming Wellness Health; a holistic lifestyle blog where she shares recipes, health tips and much more. Her love for travel and adventure brought her to Southeast Asia where she is constantly inspired by the vibrant sights, food and culture.

Andra conducts nutritional consultations from Singapore via Skype, with people from all over the world, and teaches yoga any chance she gets. She is passionate about helping her clients bring their health back into balance through healthy eating, yoga and meditation. She believes that we each have the potential to heal ourselves and be vibrant and happy each and every day.

Visit her website www.blossomingwellnesshealth.com
Instagram: @andra_cnp
Facebook: @blossomingwellnesshealth

Devina Daya is a Holistic Nutritionist and a Clinical and Counselling Psychology M.A Candidate. Her goal is to inspire, educate and contribute to a new level of consciousness - one that promotes happier, healthier and more fulfilled lives. Devina believes in the power of making healthy diet and lifestyle choices, as well as nutritional supplementation, when necessary, to enhance wellbeing. The importance of optimal nutritional status, and the power of the mind, our greatest tool, cannot be overstated as methods to help us thrive and feel our best.

For more of her favourite recipes and lifestyle tips and resources, find her at website www.devinadaya.com

Deiala Abdallah graduated with honours from Humber College: School of Hospitality and worked in plenty of restaurants in Toronto. She went on to study nutrition at the Institute of Holistic Nutrition and is a fitness enthusiast who dreams of inspiring others. The love Deiala has towards whole nutritious food and the art of movement of the body is something I wants to share with you. Knowledge, good food, love, support, and the will power to exercise is all you will need to live a healthy and happy life!

Connect with her via email to deiala.abdallah@gmail.com
Instagram: @HolisticallyFitAndFab

Acknowledgements

There are so many people that I wish to personally thank for helping me make this cookbook a reality. A huge thank you to:

Andrea Kmecza, who put so much energy into this cookbook! Her recipes are so yummy and she is a pleasure to work with. From helping me curate the recipes and testing each and every one of them, to running around the city looking for props for our photoshoot and editing the manuscript, Andrea's help was greatly appreciated.

My husband, who spent countless hours editing and designing this cookbook. He is extremely supportive of my endeavours and promised (in our wedding vows!) to provide me with constructive criticism on all of my creations.

The recipe contributors who were kind enough to allow me to publish their delicious recipes.

My mom, Margot Schelew, who tested a ton of the recipes, provided moral support and edited the manuscript.

All 30 of the recipe testers, with a special shout out to Sharon Otness, Katherine Fox, Miriam MacDonald, and Laura Stolf, who spent the summer testing the recipes and providing detailed feedback on all of the recipes so I could make them even tastier.

My amazing friends, who kindly accepted all of the desserts I forced upon them every time they visited.

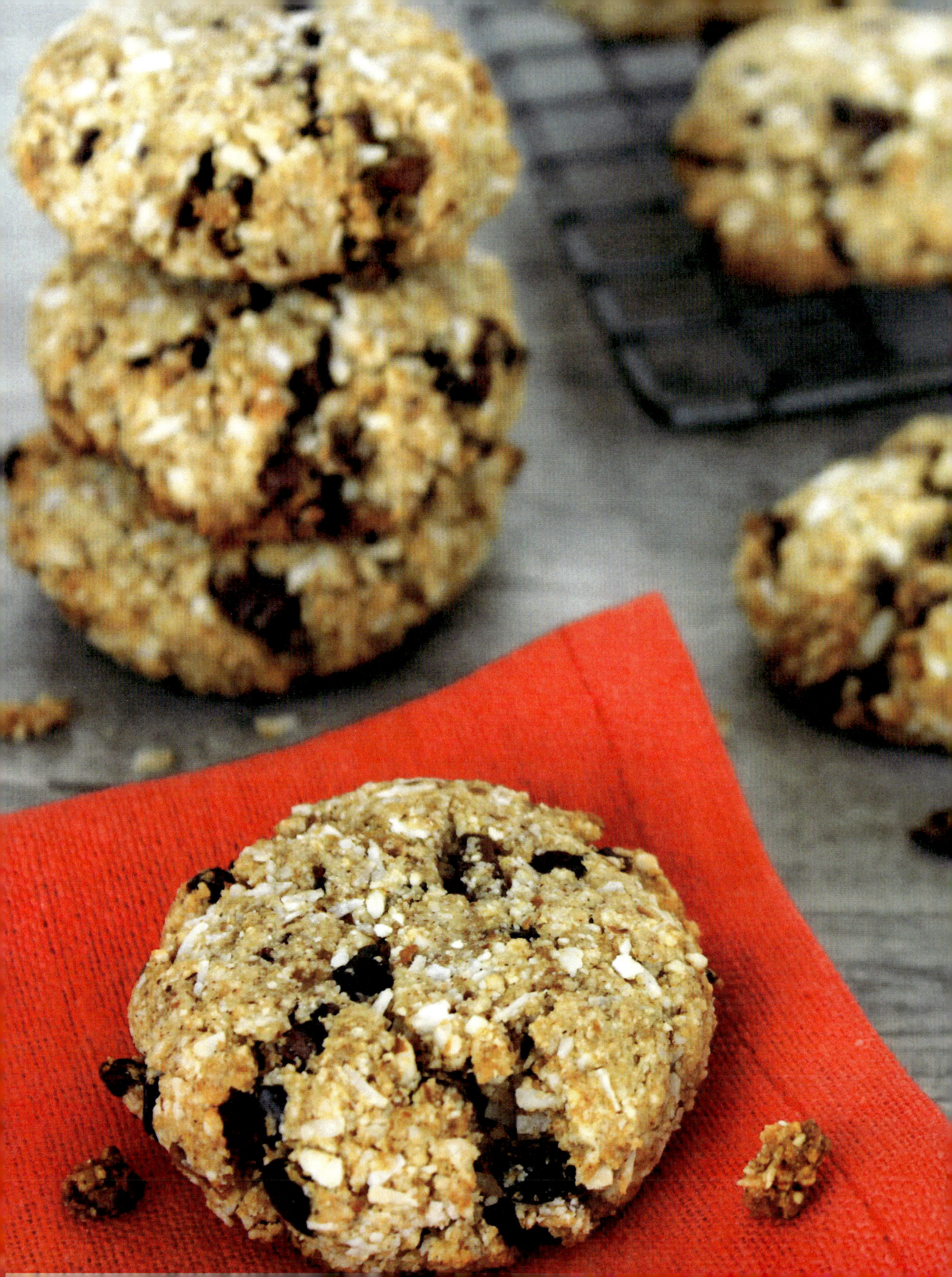

Recipes

I like to create recipes that accommodate a variety of food allergies, diets and lifestyle choices. All of the recipes in the eBook are vegetarian, dairy free and made without processed sugar or flours. Many of them are also vegan, raw, nut free, sugar free, paleo and gluten free.

V	Vegan:	Contains no animal products or honey
P	Paleo:	Free from legumes, sugar or grains
R	Raw:	Ingredients and final product have not been heated
SF	Sugar Free:	Does not contain coconut sugar, honey or maple syrup but may contain stevia and fruit
NF	Nut Free:	Does not contain nuts
GF	Gluten Free:	Does not contain any glutinous grains

Use the symbols below to easily find the recipes that fall into specific categories.

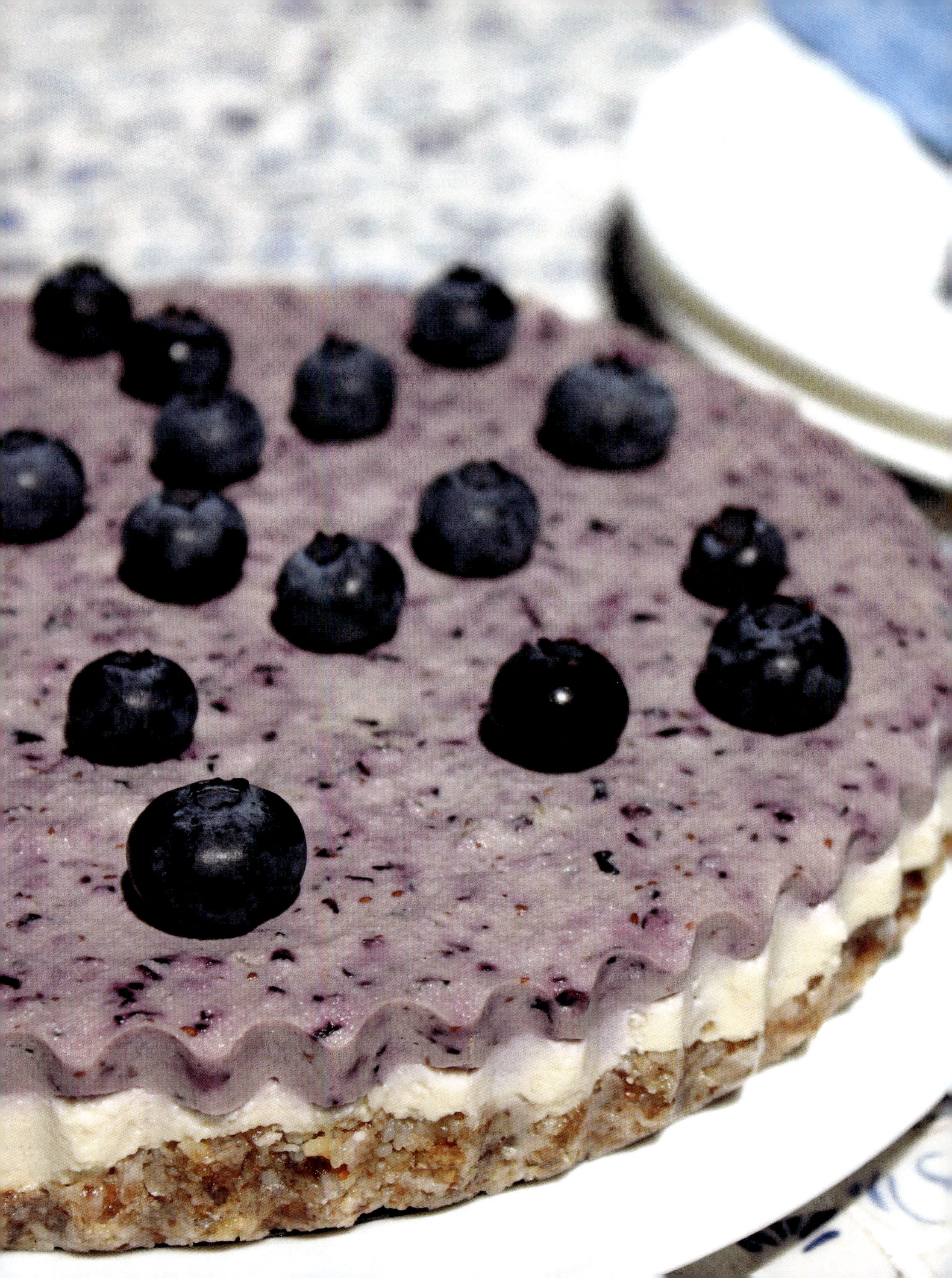

Raw Blueberry Cheesecake

(V) (R) (SF) (P) (GF)

Prep time: 20 minutes | Inactive prep time: 11 hours | Serving size: 12 slices

Raw Blueberry Cheesecake is made with a chewy gluten free date and pecan base that is topped with creamy vegan blueberry cashew cream cheese that tastes just like the real thing. It gets all of its sweetness from the dates, blueberries and a pinch of stevia making it sugar free and bursting with fiber and antioxidants.

Ingredients

- 2 cups raw cashews
- Juice of one lemon
- 1/2 tsp stevia
- 6 Tbsp coconut oil
- 1/2 tsp vanilla
- 1.5 cups wild blueberries
- 1/2 cup medjool dates, roughly 5

- 1 cup pecans
- 1/2 cup unsweetened shredded coconut
- 1/4 tsp stevia
- 1/4 tsp salt
- 2-4 tsp water *optional

Method

1. Place cashews in a bowl and cover them with water. Soak for at least 3 hours to overnight and rinse before using.
2. To make the base, place the dates, pecans, shredded coconut, stevia and salt in a high speed blender or food processor and pulse until it forms into a chunky crumbly mixture. If your dates are really dry, you may need to add 2-4 tsp of water. The base is ready when you can roll it into a ball that stays together.
3. Press the base mixture into a 7" spring form pan. Place it in the freezer to chill while you prepare the blueberry cheesecake filling.
4. To make the filling, place the soaked cashews, lemon juice, stevia, coconut oil and vanilla in the high speed blender or food processor and process until silky smooth.
5. Remove the chilled base from the freezer and top with 2/3 of the cashew cream cheese and return to the freezer to set.
6. Add 1 cup of blueberries to the remaining filling and process until smooth. Pour over the chilled cheesecake, cover and freeze until solid, roughly 5 hours.
7. Before serving, defrost the raw blueberry cheesecake in the fridge for 3 hours and garnish with the remaining 1/2 cup of blueberries.

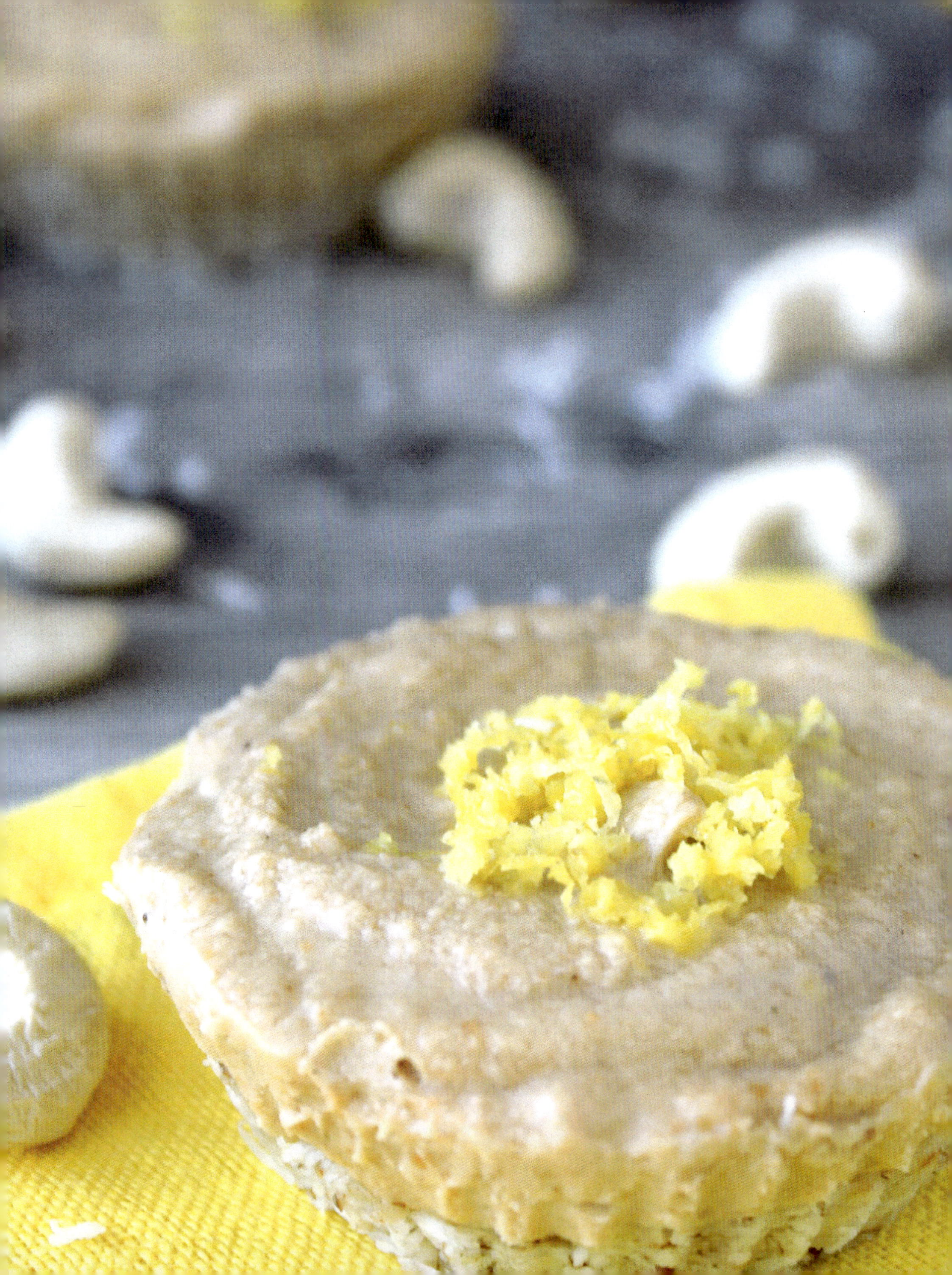

Raw Lemon Cheesecake Tarts

(V) (R) (SF) (P) (GF)

Prep time: 15 minutes | Chill time: 2 hours | Serving size: 6 full sized tarts

Raw Lemon Cheesecake Tarts are creamy and luscious with a hint of tart sourness from the lemons. The base is a gluten free mix of almonds and coconut and the silky vegan filling is made with lemons, cashew butter and sweetened with stevia.

Ingredients

Crust

- 1/2 cup almonds, raw
- 1/2 cup shredded coconut, unsweetened
- 1/8 tsp stevia
- 1/8 tsp salt
- 3 Tbsp coconut oil, melted

Filling

- Zest from 1 lemon
- Juice of 1 lemon, 4 Tbsp at room temperature
- 3/4 cup raw cashew butter, at room temperature
- 1/8 tsp stevia
- 2 Tbsp coconut oil, melted
- 1 Tbsp almond milk, at room temperature
- 1/4 tsp vanilla

Method

1. Place the almonds in a food processor and pulse until finely ground.
2. Transfer to a bowl and mix in the shredded coconut, stevia and salt.
3. Add the coconut oil and stir until mixed.
4. Press the mixture into the bottom of 6 baking cups or 12 mini cups and freeze until the filling is ready.
5. In a medium sized bowl zest one lemon and set aside 1 Tbsp of zest for garnish.
6. Add the juice from the lemon, zest, cashew butter, stevia, coconut oil and almond milk and stir until mixed.
7. Remove the chilled tarts from the freezer and evenly divide the lemon filling among the tarts and top with the lemon zest garnish. Place back in the freezer and chill for 2 hours to set.
8. Enjoy straight out of the freezer or place the tarts in the fridge for 30 minutes to soften.

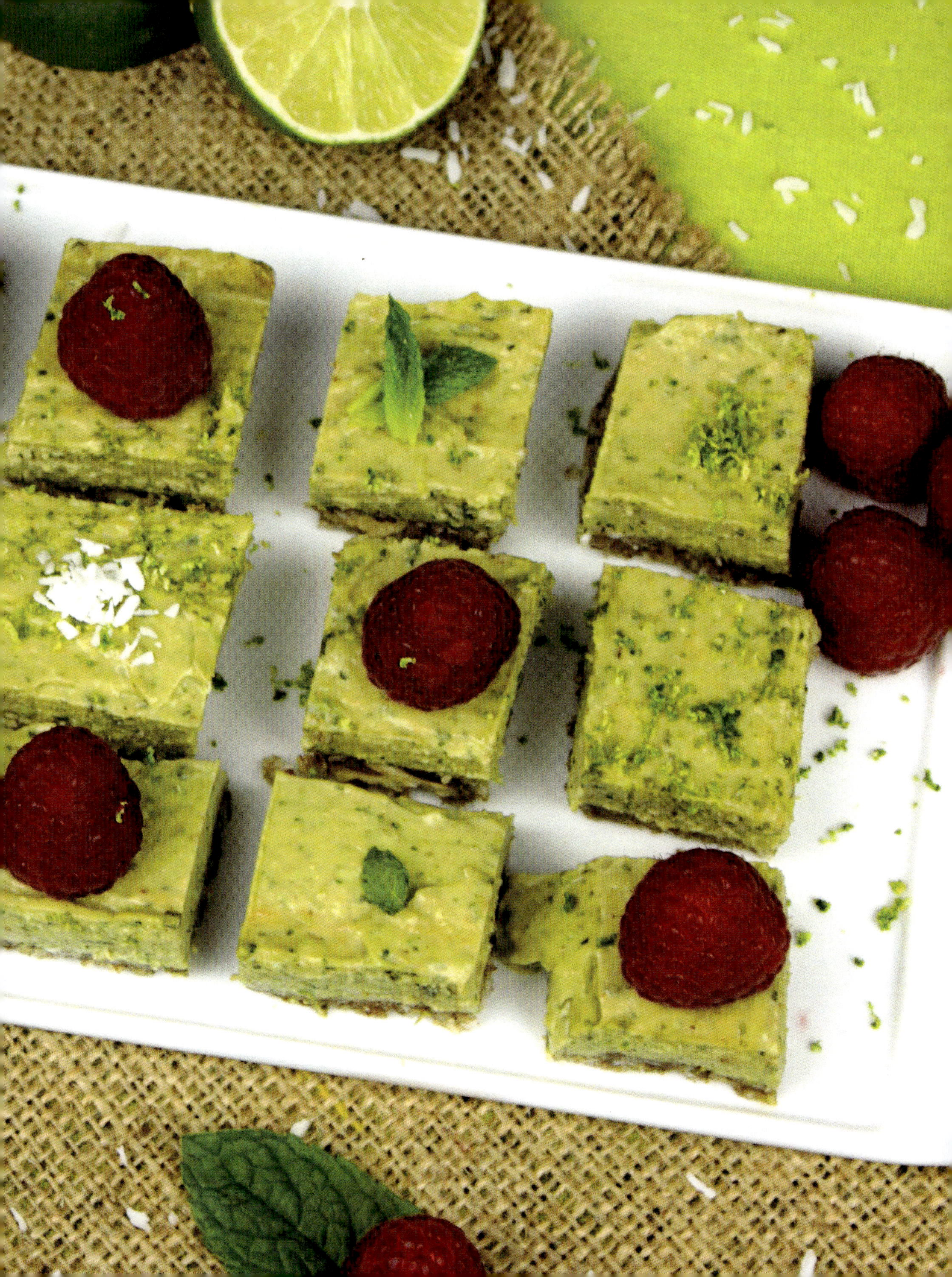

Raw Mojito Squares

(V) (R) (SF) (P) (GF)

Prep time: 15 minutes | Chill time: 2 hours | Serving size: 16 squares

Raw Mojito Squares are the perfect summer dessert because they don't require cooking and they are cool and refreshing. I love them because they are sugar free getting all of their sweetness from stevia, so they are perfect for people on the candida diet.

Ingredients

Gluten-Free Crust

- 2 cup pecans, raw
- 1/2 cup shredded coconut, unsweetened
- 1/4 tsp stevia
- 1/4 tsp salt
- 1/2 tsp vanilla
- 6 Tbsp coconut oil, melted

Filling

- 2 limes, zested and juiced (6 Tbsp of juice at room temperature)
- 1 soft avocado, roughly diced
- 1/2 cup raw cashew butter, at room temperature
- 1/2 cup fresh mint leaves, chopped
- 1/4 tsp powdered stevia (to taste)
- 1 tsp mint extract
- 3 Tbsp melted coconut oil, melted
- 1 cup raspberries

Method

1. Place the pecans in a food processor and pulse until finely ground.
2. Transfer to a bowl and mix in the shredded coconut, stevia and salt.
3. Add the coconut oil and vanilla and stir until mixed.
4. Press the mixture into the bottom 8×8 pan lined with wax paper and freeze until the filling is ready.
5. In a medium sized bowl, zest 2 limes and set aside 2 Tbsp of zest for garnish.
6. In a food processor process the zest, lime juice, avocado, cashew butter, mint, stevia, mint extract and coconut oil and process until silky smooth.
7. Remove the chilled crust from the freezer spread the filling over the top then sprinkle with the remaining zest. Place in the freezer and chill for 2 hours to set.
8. Before serving, place the Raw Mojito Squares on the counter for 20 minutes or in the fridge for 2 hours to soften. Then top with fresh raspberries and serve.

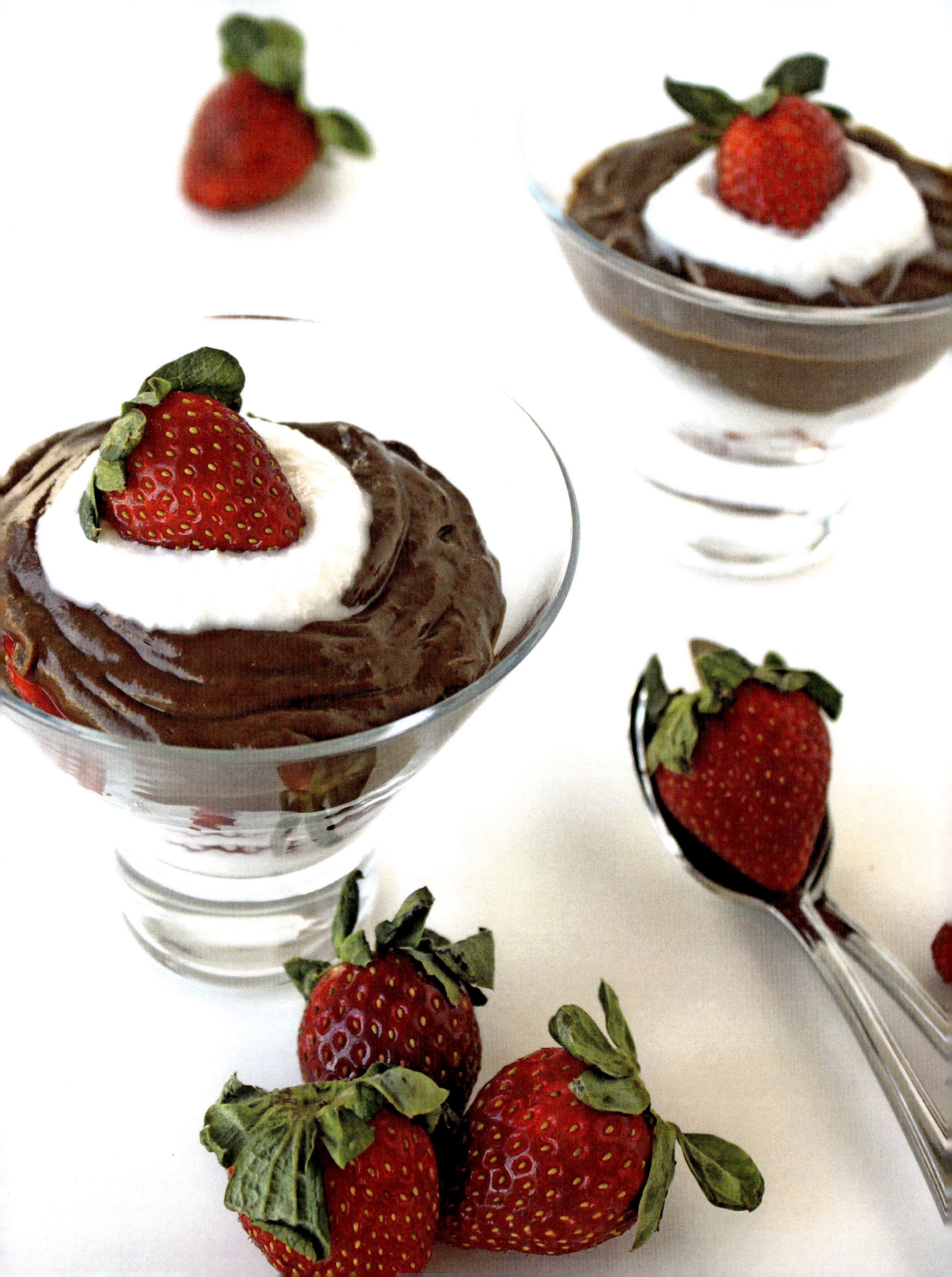

Chocolate Avocado Pudding

(V) (NF) (GF)

Prep time: 2 minutes | Serving size: 3

Chocolate avocado pudding is a thick and creamy dessert that tastes indulgent, but it is actually healthy. It taste just like instant chocolate pudding in a good way – you would never guess the main ingredient is avocado! In addition to being a rich pudding, it can also be enjoyed as a delicious fruit or berry dip or used as icing.

Ingredients

- 1 avocado
- 3 Tbsp raw cacao powder
- 1/2 tsp vanilla
- 1/4 cup maple syrup
- 1 tsp cinnamon
- 2 Tbsp milk alternative

Method

1. Combine all ingredients into a blender or food processor. Blend well until smooth and enjoy!

Health Benefits of Avocados

Avocados are filled with healthy fats that you don't have to be afraid of because they provide powerful anti-inflammatory properties and don't make you fat. Avocados also contain oleic acid which is a healthy fat that helps with the absorption of fat soluble nutrients like vitamin A, D E and K. Avocados are very high in carotenoids which our body can convert to vitamin A to nourish your eyes. The fibre found in avocados slows the release of sugar into your system so you don't get a sugar crash after enjoying this decadent dessert.

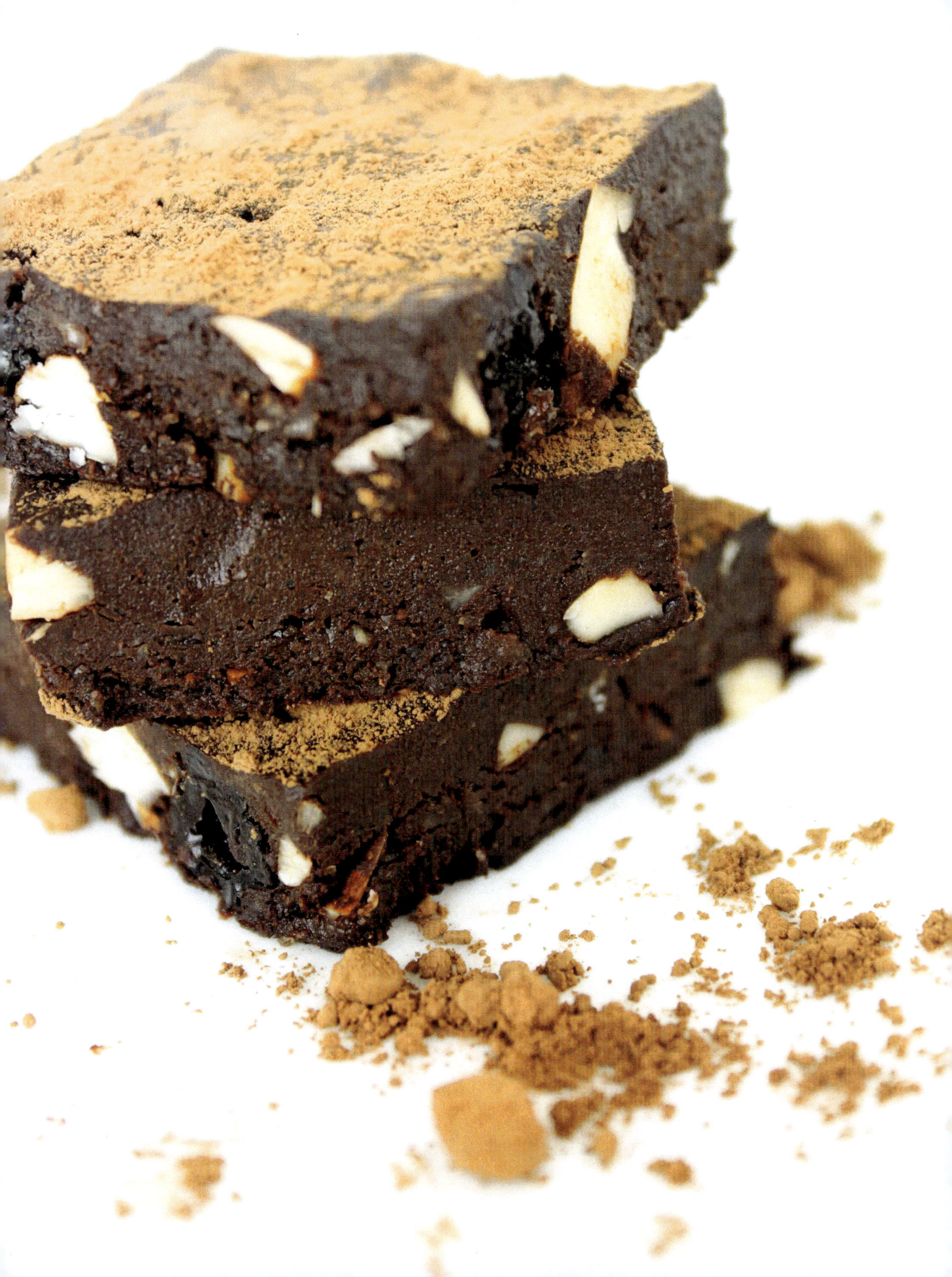

Black Forest Brownies

V R SF P GF

Soaking time: 1 hour | Prep time: 10 minutes | Chill time: 2 hours

Black Forest Brownies are a decadent chocolate cherry dessert that are raw and vegan. They are naturally sweetened with dates and cherries which create a smooth and rich brownie filled with crunchy almonds and chewy cherries for added texture. Black Forest Brownies only contain 6 ingredients and they are really easy to make.

Ingredients

- 1 1/2 cups dried cherries
- 2 cups walnuts
- 1 cup raw cacao powder
- 1/4 teaspoons salt
- 1/2 cup medjool dates (roughly 4)
- 1/2 almonds, chopped

Method

1. Soak 1 cup of cherries in water for an hour.
2. Place 2 cups of walnuts in a food processor and process into a granular flour.
3. Add 1 cup of cacao powder and 1/4 teaspoons of salt to the food processor and process until smooth.
4. While the food processor is running, slowly add 1 cup of soaked cherries and 1/2 cup of dates and process until smooth.
5. Fold in 1/2 cup of cherries and 1/2 cup of raw chopped almonds.
6. Press the brownie batter into lined 8×8 brownie pan and freeze for 2 hours to set the brownies.
7. Remove from the freezer and cut 8-12 brownies and serve.

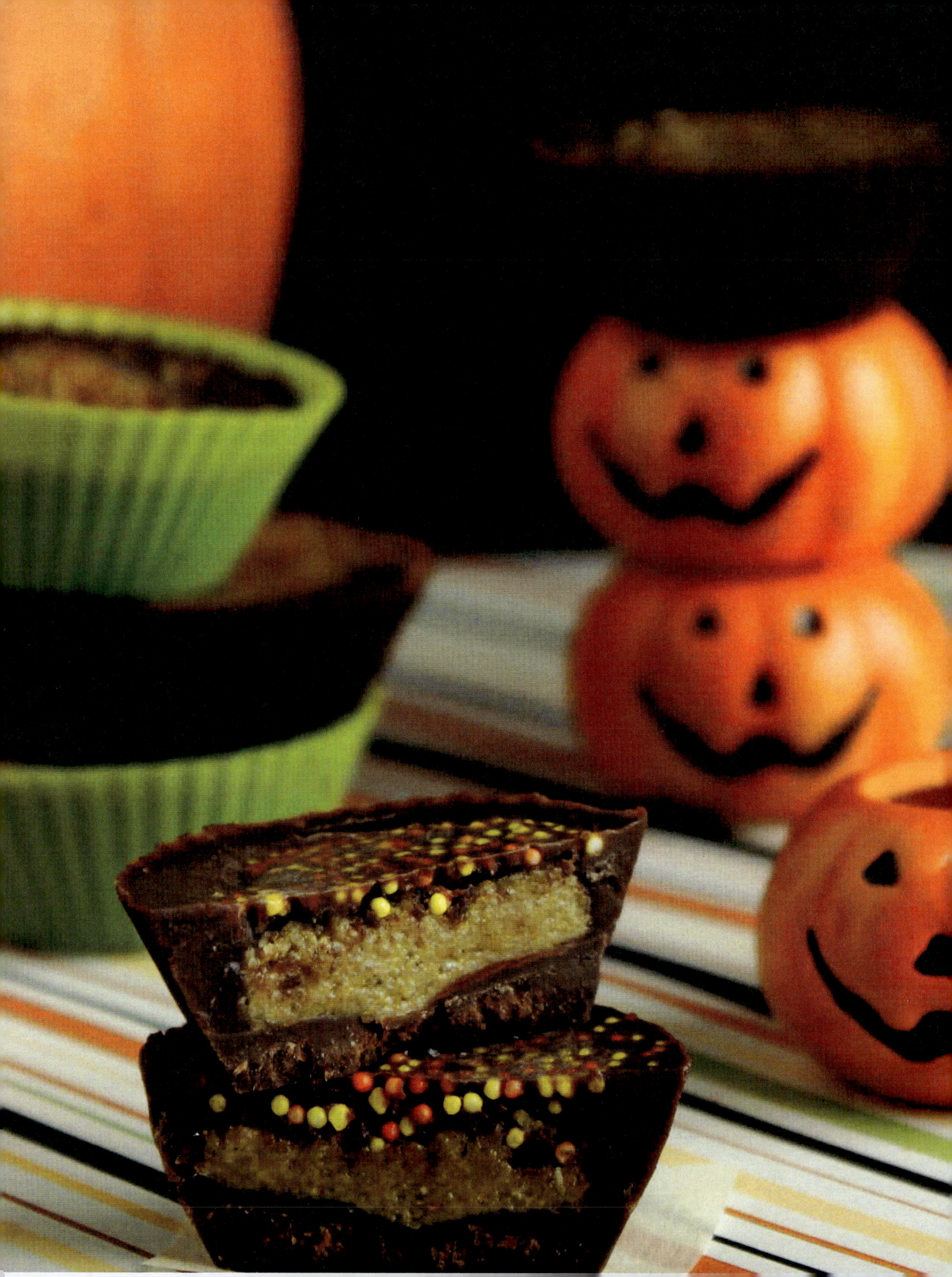

Healthy Pea(not) Butter Cups

Prep time: 10 minutes | Chill Time: 2 hours | Serving Size: 6 large or 12 small cups

Healthy Pea(not) Butter Cups melt in your mouth and are a million times better than the processed sugar laden version. They have a creamy sunflower seed butter center that is nestled in a stevia sweetened carob shell. If you have never tried sunflower seed butter or carob, you will find that they are a match made in heaven.

Ingredients

Carob Shell

- 1/2 cup coconut oil, melted
- 1/2 cup carob, sifted
- 15 drops liquid stevia
- 1/4 tsp vanilla

Sunflower Seed Filling

- 3 Tbsp sunflower seed butter
- 1 1/2 Tbsp nutritional yeast
- 1-3 Tbsp coconut flour
- 1/4 tsp powdered stevia
- pinch salt

Method

1. To make the carob shell, whisk the melted coconut oil, carob powder, stevia and vanilla together in a small bowl.
2. Pour a third of the carob shell mixture into a muffin pan lined with paper or silicone liners and place in the freezer to set.
3. While the base is hardening, make the filling by stirring together the sunflower seed butter, nutritional yeast, 1 Tbsp coconut flour, stevia and salt. Depending on the consistency of the sunflower seed butter you are using, add additional coconut flour until the filling becomes a wet dough.
4. Remove the muffin pan from the freezer and roll the filling into balls. Place a ball into each base and flatten it into a smooth disk.
5. Top with the remaining carob shell mixture and freeze for 2 hours to set.
6. Store in the freezer in an air tight container and serve cold.

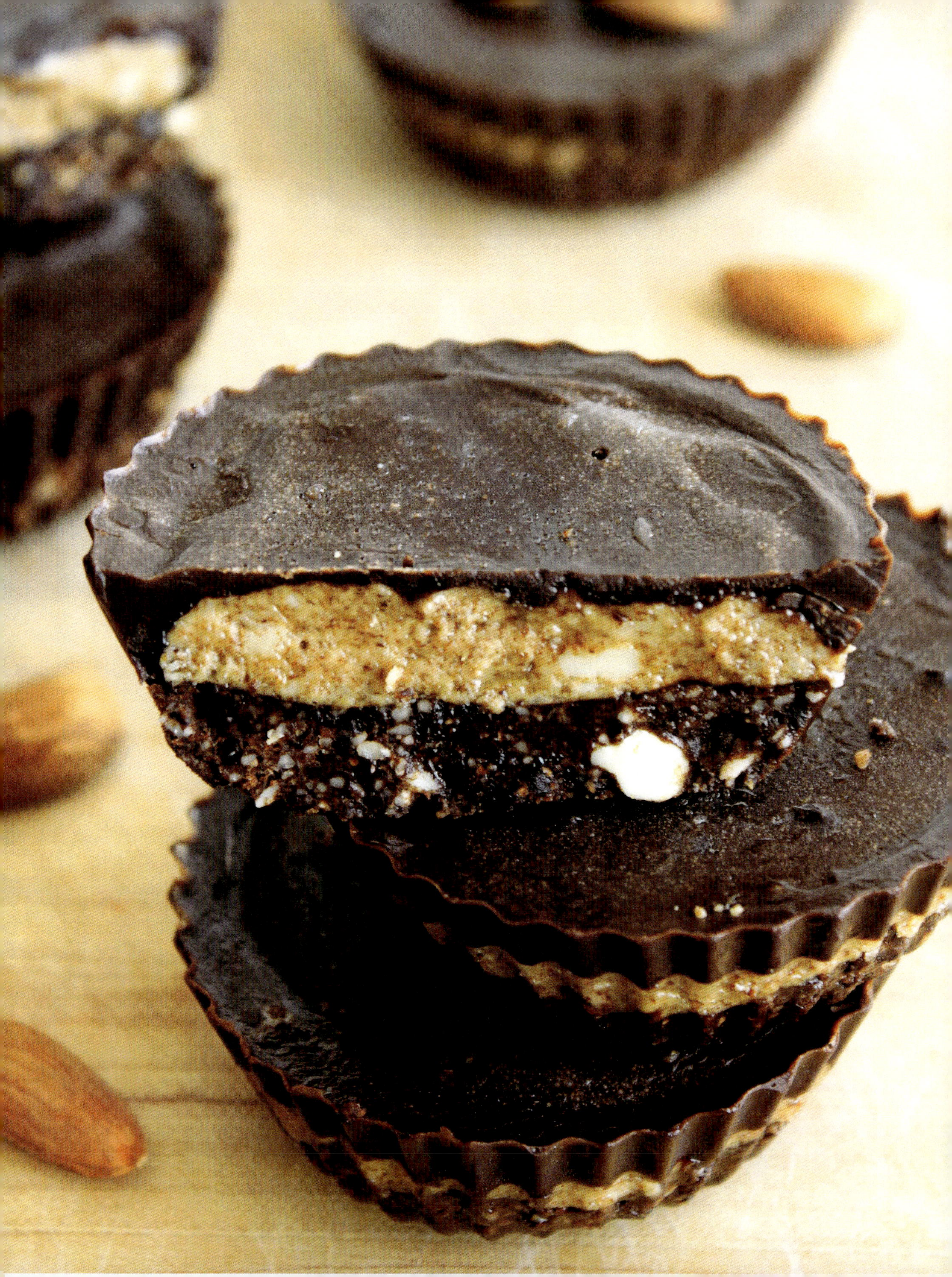

Almond Carob Tarts

P SF GF

Prep: 25 minutes | Inactive prep: 2 hours | Serving size: 6

These decadent melt-in-your-mouth tarts are the perfect way to satisfy your sweet tooth. They are packed with healthy fats, lots of protein and sweetened with stevia making them a delicious guilt free dessert. You can enjoy these as a yummy evening treat because they are made with carob instead of chocolate so they don't contain caffeine. I like to keep some in my freezer so when my sugar buster cravings hit I have something healthy to reach for.

Ingredients

Base
- 1/2 cup raw almonds
- 1/2 cup carob powder
- 1/8 tsp stevia powder
- 5 Tbsp coconut oil, melted

Topping
- 3 Tbsp melted coconut oil
- 3 Tbsp carob powder
- 1/8 tsp stevia powder
- 1/2 cup strawberries *optional
- Sprinkle of salt

Filling
- 3/4 cup almond butter
- 1/8 tsp stevia
- 3 Tbsp almond flour
- 1 Tbsp nutritional yeast

Method

1. To make the base, place almonds in a food processor and blend until finely chopped. Add additional base ingredients and pulse until mixed. Divide the base into 6 and press into 6 muffin liners then place in the freezer to set.
2. To make the filing mix together the filling ingredients by hand or in a blender until smooth. Divide into 6 and spoon over the chilled bases, smoothing the top with the back of a spoon. Return to the freezer to set.
3. At this point you have the option to add the strawberries. First blend them until smooth then divide into 6, spoon over the chilled bases and return to the freezer to set.
4. To make the topping, whisk or blend together the ingredients until smooth. Pour over the chilled almond carob tarts and return back to the freezer for 2 hours to set.
5. Store in the freezer and enjoy straight out of the freezer or gently thaw on the counter for 20 minutes or in the fridge for 1 hour.

Share your creations with #JLWCookbook | Recipe by: Jesse Lane Lee

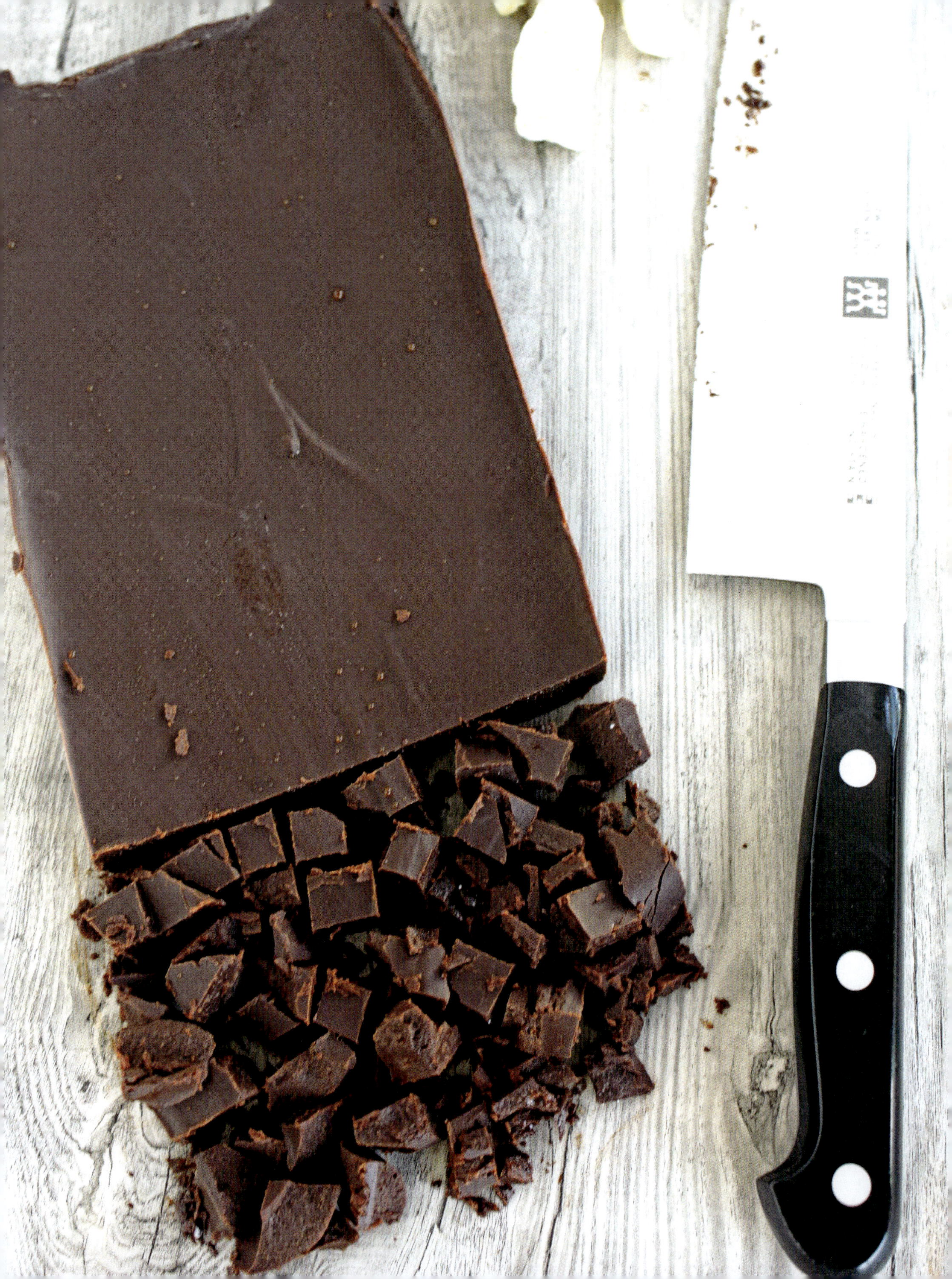

Homemade Chocolate Bar

(V) (R) (SF) (P) (GF)

Prep time: 15 minutes | Inactive prep time: 2 hours and overnight* | Serving size: 1 large bar!

Making your own chocolate isn't actually that hard and it is kinda fun too! You can enjoy this recipe as it, or cut it up into chocolate chunks that can be substituted for chocolate chips in any of the recipes in this cookbook. You can also play around with it by adding essential oils, nuts, seeds and dried fruit.

Ingredients

- 1 cup cacao butter
- 1 cup raw cacao powder, sifted to remove lumps
- 1/2 cup maple syrup
- 1 tsp vanilla

Method

1. Melt cacao butter in a double broiler or glass bowl on top of a pot of water (make sure the bowl isn't touching the water) over medium heat.
2. When the cacao butter is melted, remove from the heat and whisk in the remaining ingredients.
3. Pour the chocolate into a bread pan lined with parchment paper and place in the fridge to harden.
4. Once it is hard you can cut it into chocolate chunks or enjoy as is.

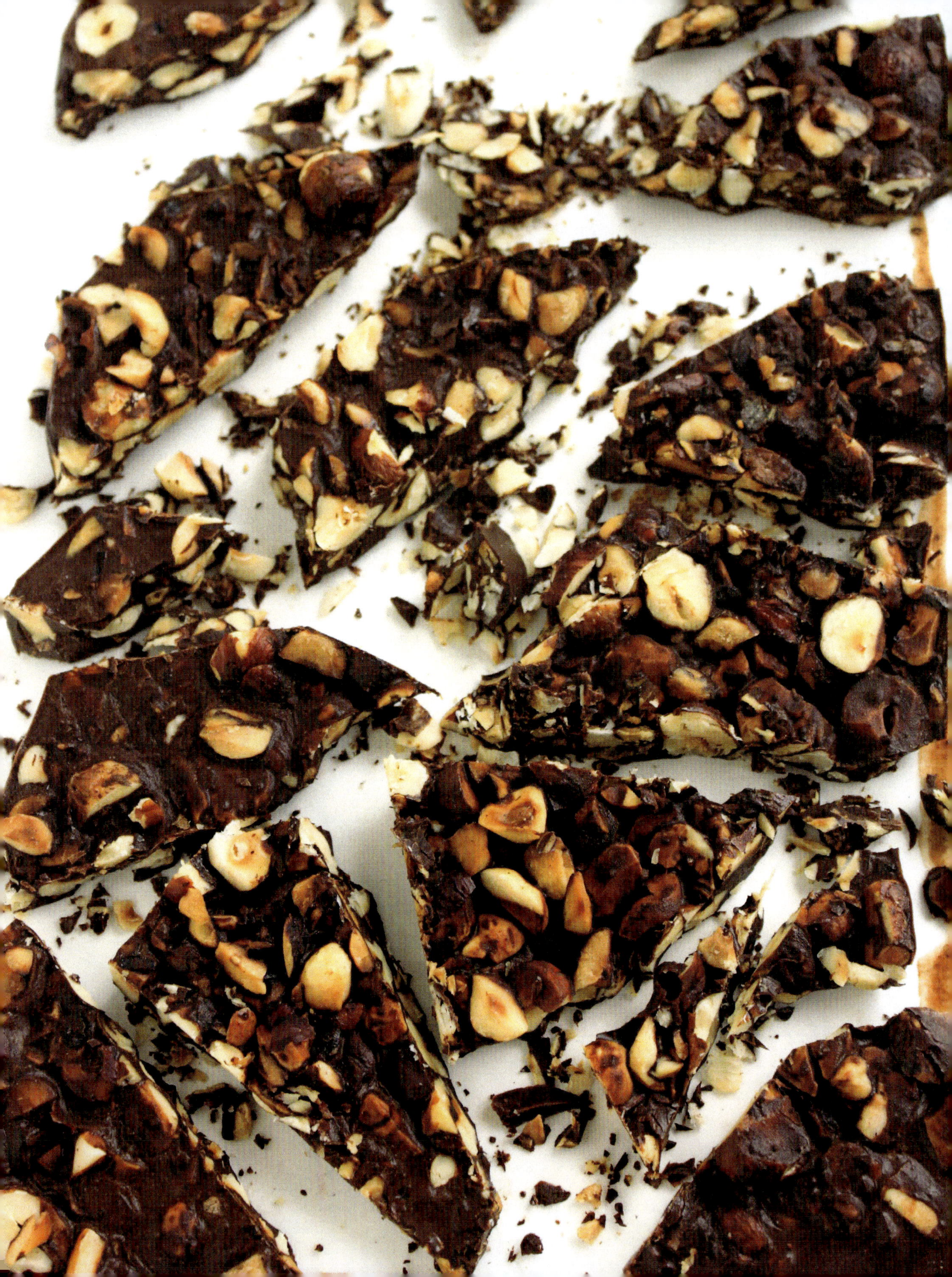

Carob Hazelnut Bark

(V) (SF) (P) (GF)

Prep time: 15 minutes | Inactive prep time: 2 hours and overnight* | Serving size: 1 large bar!

I LOVE chocolate bark but it can be packed with lots of unhealthy ingredients and tons of sugar, so I decided to create my own version! Carob Hazelnut Bark melts in your mouth and the toasted hazelnut pieces sprinkled throughout the bark bring a satisfying crunch. The base of the carob bark is actually super healthy and, if you don't like hazelnuts, you can play around with the recipe by adding different types of nuts, seeds and/or dried fruit.

Ingredients

- 1 cup hazelnuts, chopped
- 1 cup carob powder, sifted
- 1/8 tsp green powder stevia
- 1/2 cup coconut oil, melted

Method

1. Place chopped hazelnuts in a dry frying pan on medium high heat. Toast until golden brown and fragrant.
2. Line a loaf pan with parchment paper and evenly spread ¾ of the nuts along the bottom of the pan.
3. In a medium bowl mix the carob and stevia powder. Add the coconut oil and stir until smooth; this mixture should be very drippy.
4. Pour the chocolate into the pan sprinkle with the remaining hazelnuts. Place in the freezer to set for 2 hours.
5. Serve cold, straight out of the freezer. Do not leave at room temperature for too long or else it may start to melt!

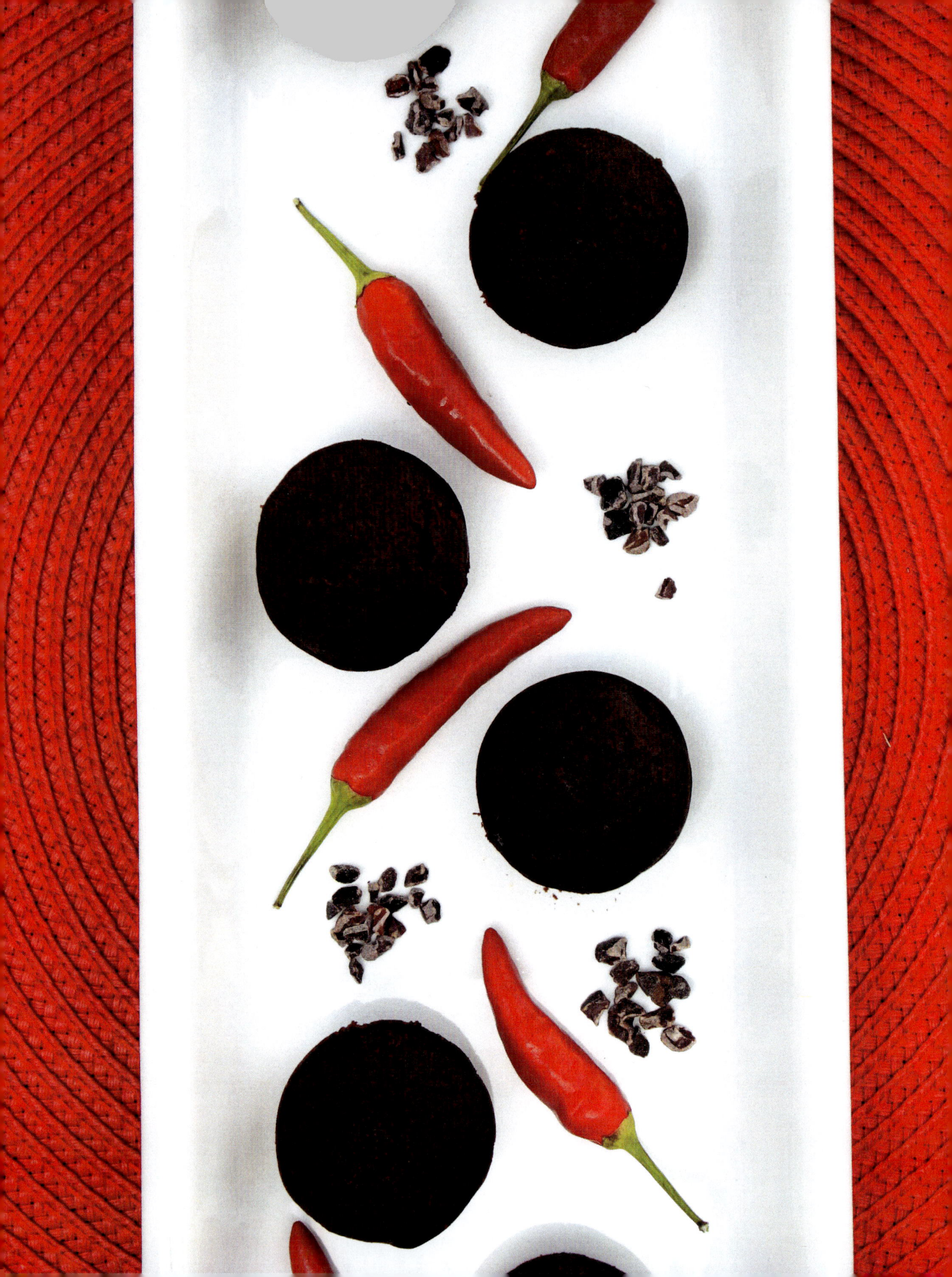

Dark Chocolate Chili Bites

NF P GF

Prep time: 20 minutes | Cooking time: 10 minutes | Serving size: 30-35 bites

As a Holistic Nutritionist I try to make healthy choices with all my meals, but I still want to have my cake and eat it too!! Well now you can have this treat guilt-free. I adapted this recipe which is simple to make and the ingredients can be cut in half or doubled very easily, depending on the quantity you want to make. The other great thing about this recipe is that the measurements don't have to be exact, so don't worry about fussing over whether you have added too much chocolate or not enough coconut oil.

Ingredients

- 200g organic dark chocolate 3/4 cup organic virgin coconut oil
- 3/4 cup organic coconut sugar
- 1 Tbsp coconut flour
- 4 large organic eggs
- 1 tsp chili powder
- 1/4 tsp cayenne powder
- 1/2 cup cacao nibs *optional
- Pinch salt

Method

1. Preheat the oven to 400°F.
2. Melt the coconut oil and chocolate in a small saucepan over low heat.
3. Pour the melted coconut oil and chocolate into a mixing bowl.
4. Add sugar and stir until mixed with a wooden spoon. Allow the mixture to cool.
5. Add the eggs one at a time, mixing well. If you are using an egg substitute, you may add it all at once, mixing thoroughly.
6. Stir in the flour, chili, cayenne, salt and mix well. Fold in mini chocolate chips or cacao nibs if using.
7. Lightly grease a mini muffin tin with coconut oil and pour the mixture into pan about 3/4 full. Bake for 10-12 minutes.
8. Allow mini bites to cool before removing from pan, then transfer onto a wire rack to cool completely.
9. They taste the best at room temperature. Store remainder in airtight container and refrigerate. Remove from fridge about an hour before serving. They can also be frozen for up to one month, but they are so yummy they won't last that long!

Share your creations with #JLWCookbook | Recipe by: Andrea Kmecza

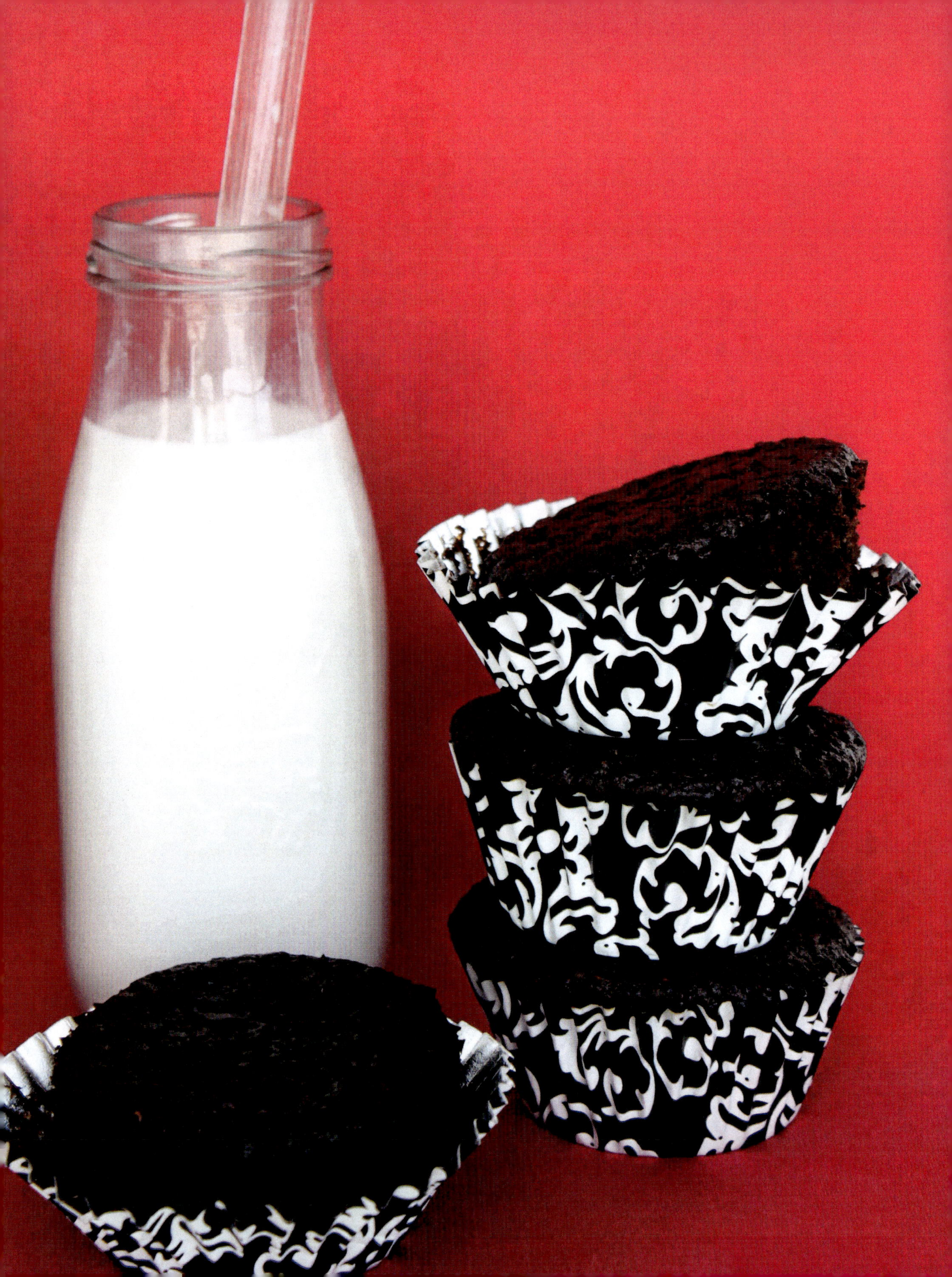

Quinoa Cocoa Cupcakes

Prep time: 15 minutes | Cook time: 30 minutes | Serving size: 12 cupcakes

These chocolate cupcakes are really unique and very easy to throw together. They are super moist and have an intense chocolaty flavour. They are a perfect way to use up extra cooked quinoa and taste even better after a night in the fridge.

Ingredients

- 2/3 cup of uncooked quinoa (2 cups already cooked quinoa)
- 1 1/2 cups of filtered water
- 1/2 cup of unsweetened almond milk
- 4 eggs
- 2 Tbsp vanilla (or more to taste)
- 1/3 cup of melted coconut oil
- 1/2 cup honey
- 1 cup unsweetened cocoa powder (use more or less to your liking)
- 1 Tbsp baking powder
- 1/4 tsp salt

Method

1. Cook quinoa in water - bring water to a boil, add quinoa and bring to a boil once more. Cover, lower heat and simmer for about 10 minutes. Once cooked, allow time to completely cool.
2. Preheat oven to 350F degrees and line a cupcake tray with parchment paper baking cups.
3. Mix eggs, vanilla, milk, honey and coconut oil in a bowl, add quinoa.
4. In a separate bowl mix cocoa powder, salt and baking powder together.
5. Add to wet mixture and stir.
6. Pour into cupcake tray and bake for 20 minutes.

Share your creations with #JLWCookbook | Recipe by: Lynsey Franklin

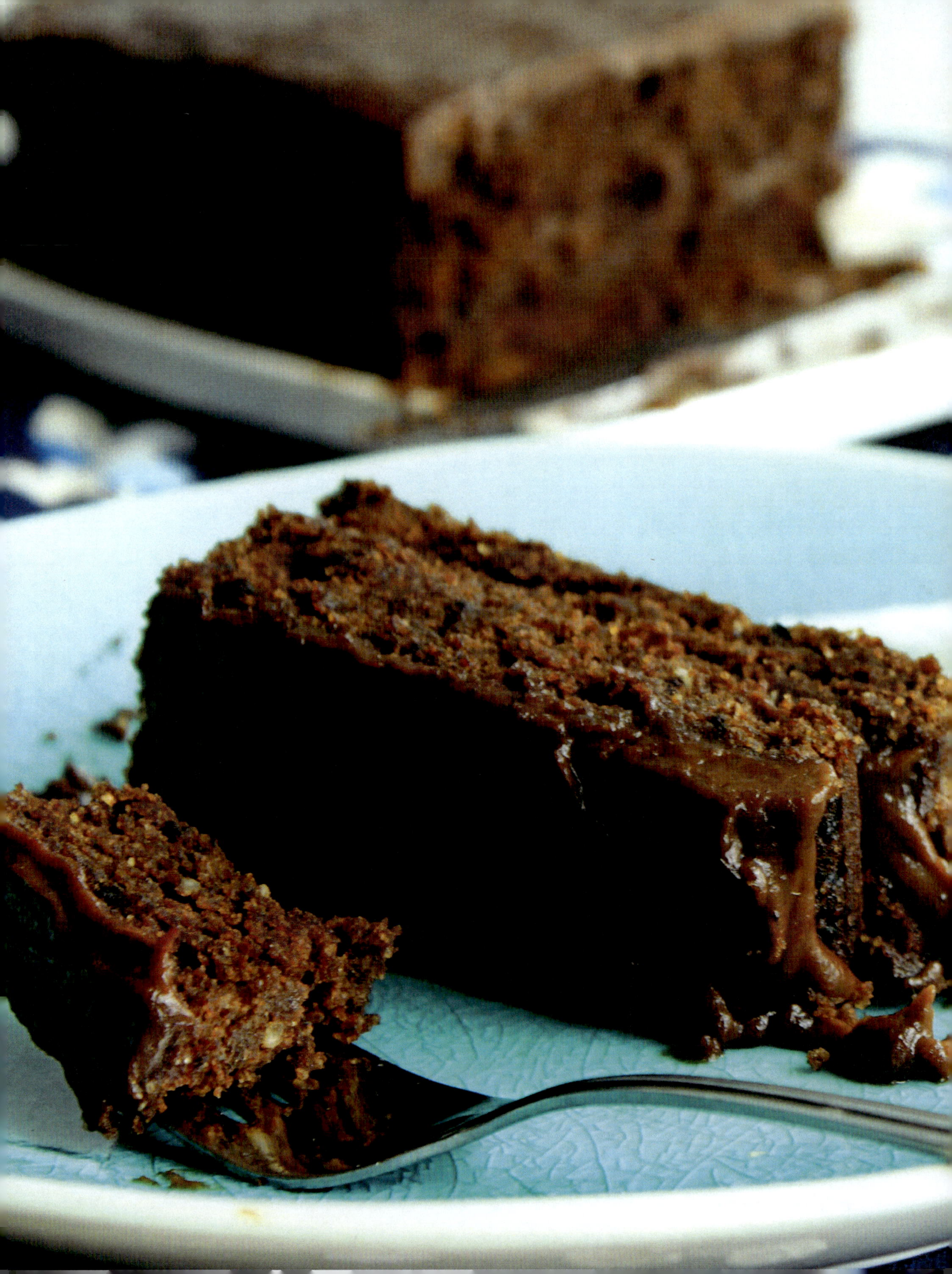

Carob Cake with Fudge Icing

P | GF

Prep time: 10 minutes | Cook time: 20 minutes | Serving Size: 8

Carob Cake with Fudge Icing is a moist layered chocolaty cake slathered in gooey fudge icing. The cake is made with almond flour making it gluten free and paleo. The creation of this chocolaty gluten free carob cake was no accident, my husband and I were grocery shopping and he wanted to buy a McCain's Deep and Delicious Cake. I took a peek at the ingredients and what I saw didn't surprise me: lots and lots of sugar, gluten, dairy, processed oil and genetically modified ingredients. I knew I could make a healthier version that tasted even better!

Ingredients

Carob Cake

- 1/2 cup carob powder
- 1/2 cup almond flour
- 1/4 cup coconut flour
- 1/8 tsp salt
- 1/2 tsp baking powder
- 1/2 cup melted coconut oil
- 1/2 cup maple syrup (at room temperature)
- 2 eggs (at room temperature)
- 2 tsp vanilla

Fudgy Icing

- 10 medjool dates
- 3 Tbsp carob powder
- 3 Tbsp melted coconut oil
- 2 tsp cinnamon
- 1 tsp vanilla
- 15 drops stevia *optional
- 6 Tbsp date soaking water

Method

1. Preheat the oven to 350F and line an 8×8 baking dish with parchment paper.
2. Mix the carob powder, almond flour, coconut flour, salt and baking powder in a large bowl.
3. In a medium size bowl mix the melted coconut oil, room temperature maple syrup, eggs and vanilla. It is important that the eggs and maple syrup are at room temperature, otherwise the coconut oil will harden and clump.
4. Add the wet ingredients to the dry ingredients and whisk until smooth and mixed.
5. Pour the carob cake batter into the baking dish and bake for 20 minutes or until a toothpick inserted in the center comes out clean.
6. Soak the dates in water for 30 minutes to soften them.
7. Place the dates, carob powder, coconut oil, cinnamon, vanilla and stevia in a food processor and blend until smooth. Slowly add the water the dates soaked in until the icing is a fudge consistency, roughly 3-6 Tbsp of water.
8. Once the carob cake has cooled, cut it in half and slather the bottom layer with fudge icing. Place the next layer on top and cover it with icing and serve.

Share your creations with #JLWCookbook | Recipe by: Jesse Lane Lee

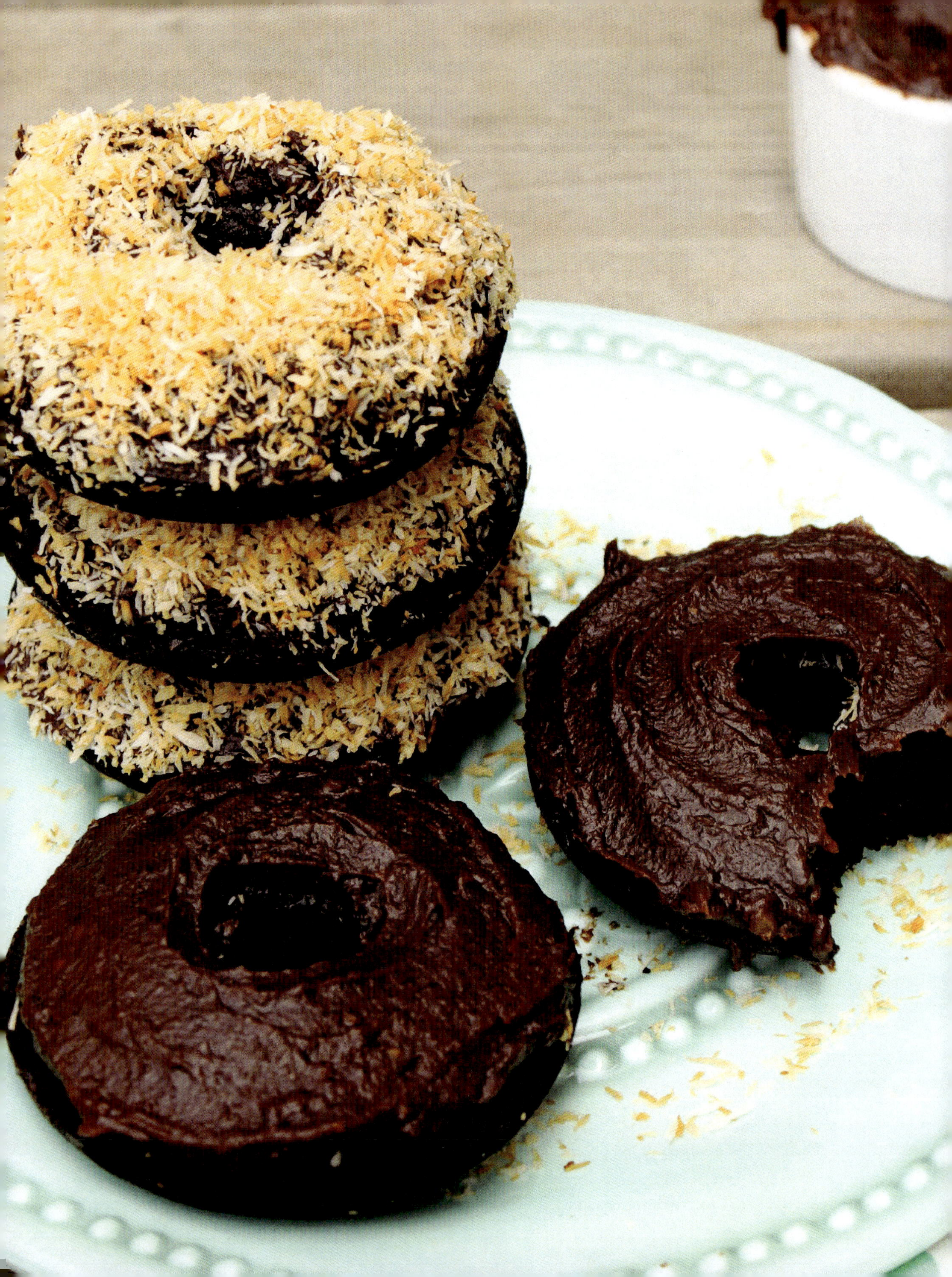

You wish Tim Horton's Donuts

NF P GF

Prep time: 15 minutes | Cook time: 20 minutes | Serving Size: 6 doughnuts

When I was a kid donuts were a regular treat around my house, so when the dirty dozen in the slender brown box from Tim Horton's made an appearance, not going to lie, it was the highlight of my day. So when I developed an allergy to gluten and dairy, I knew one of the first things I wanted to master was a donut, but this donut was going to be delicious and good for you. These donuts come fully equipped with a fudgy date frosting and dare I say, they're so healthy you could probably eat them for breakfast, take that Tim Horton's.

Ingredients

Chocolate Donuts
- 1/4 cup coconut flour
- 1/4 cup cocoa
- 1/4 tsp salt
- 1/2 tsp baking soda
- 3 eggs
- 1/4 cup maple syrup
- 1/4 cup coconut oil (melted)
- 1 Tbsp vanilla
- 1/4 cup dark chocolate chips (optional but HIGHLY recommended)

Chocolate Icing
- 1 cup of pitted dates (about 6 large medjool dates)
- 1/4 cup cocoa
- 1/4 cup coconut oil (no need to melt)
- 1/3 cup hot water

Method

1. Preheat oven to 350F and grease your donut pan with a little bit of coconut oil and set aside.
2. In a large bowl mix all the dry ingredients together until well combined.
3. In a separate bowl beat the eggs and maple syrup for about a minute (need to get some air up in there). Throw them in with the dry ingredients, add in the coconut oil and vanilla and beat until everything is good and mixed up.
4. Place the batter into a large Ziploc bag (this is my make shift piping bag) and evenly distribute the batter into your donut pan.
5. Bake in the oven for about 18-20 minutes. Once cooled these should be super easy to just twist out of the pan.
6. Toss everything into a food processor and blend until it becomes a smooth velvety texture. I popped mine into the fridge for about 10 minutes mid blend then pulsed it a few more times just for good measure.
7. Then frost away and enjoy…
8. The great thing about this recipe is that if you don't own a donut pan then just bake them off in a 9-inch square dish and this donut recipe is instantly turned into a chocolate fudge brownie.

Share your creations with #JLWCookbook | Recipe by: Alexis Nilsen

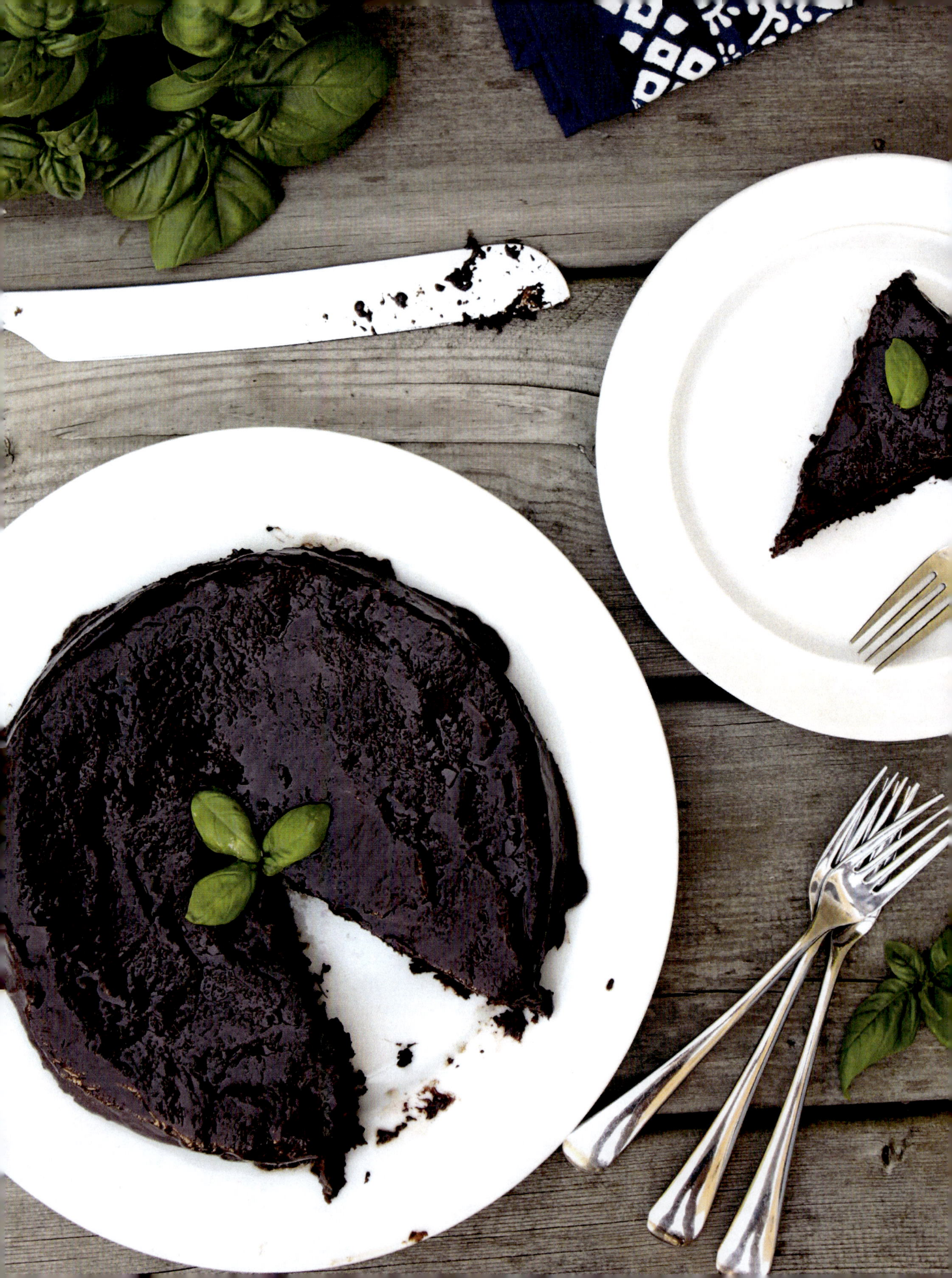

Chocolate Basil Cake

P GF

Prep time: 20 minutes | Cooking time: 20 minutes | Serving size: 8 slices

Yes, chocolate and basil, it's a delectable combination! The first time I had something similar was at a friend's house. It was in a pie version and I wanted to come up with my own gluten-free and healthier version which I've adapted from various sources over the years to get it just right.

Ingredients

Chocolate Donuts

- 3/4 cup maple sugar
- 1 cup of basil, leaves only and lightly packed
- 1/2 cup coconut oil
- 1/2 cup (100g) dark chocolate (min 70%)
- 1 tsp vanilla
- 3 large free-run organic eggs
- 1/2 cup raw cacao
- pinch of sea salt

Fudgy Date Frosting

- 1/2 cup (100g) dark chocolate (min. 70%)
- 1/3 cup coconut cream or canned full fat coconut milk

Method

1. Preheat oven to 375F.
2. Grease and 8-inch cake pan with coconut oil and line with parchment paper.
3. Add basil and sugar in a food processor and pulse until basil is very fine, mixture will look wet and pretty. Set aside.
4. Break up the chocolate into small pieces and add it into a small saucepan along with coconut oil and melt over low heat.
5. Transfer to a large mixing bowl and add the vanilla, salt and basil and whisk until smooth.
6. Now, whisk in 1 egg at a time until completely blended. Sift in the raw cacao and fold until well blended and no lumps are seen.
7. Pour the batter into the cake pan and smooth out the top and bake for 20-25 minutes. Insert a toothpick and check that the middle is baked.
8. Make your "icing" by heating the coconut cream and chocolate in a saucepan on low heat until chocolate is completely melted, stirring constantly. Remove from heat and allow it to cool a little.
9. Remove your cake form the pan and place it on serving plate. (I just flip it upside down on the plate). Pour the "icing" over it and spread with a spatula on top, letting it drip on sides. It does not have to look perfect! Garnish with basil.

Store in fridge and take out 1 hour before serving. You can also cover and store it on counter for up to 4 days, but it is so yummy it won't last that long!!!

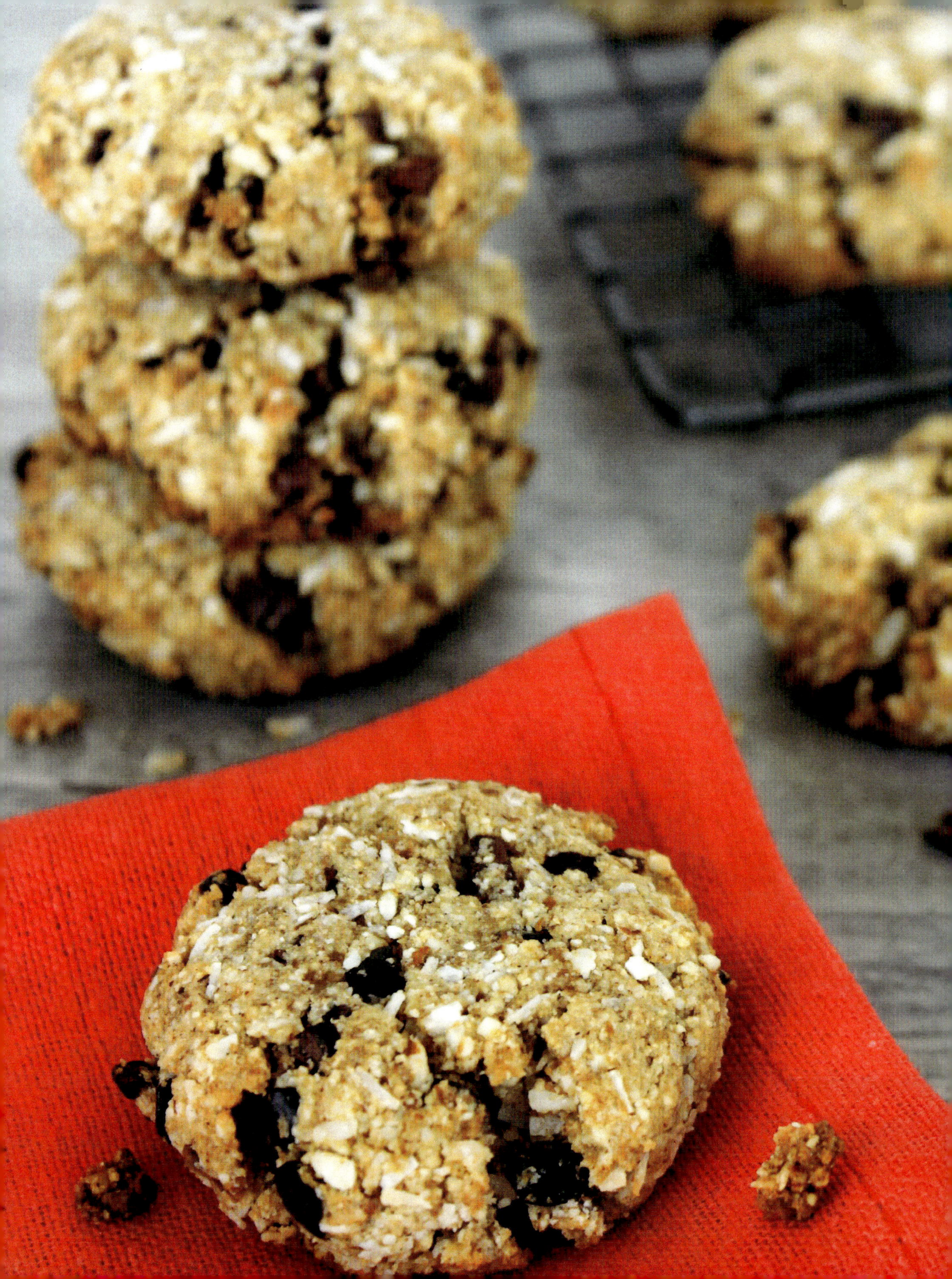

Almond Coconut Choco Chip Cookies

Prep time: 15 minutes | Inactive prep: 30 minutes | Cook time: 10 minutes | Serving size: 12

I love these cookies! They are super easy to make and are a delicious combination of almonds, chocolate and coconut. They have a fabulous texture and are the perfect amount of sweetness.

Ingredients

- 1 1/4 cups almond meal
- 1/4 cup chopped dairy-free chocolate chips or cacao nibs
- 1/2 cup shredded unsweetened coconut
- 1/2 tsp baking powder
- 1/8 teaspoon sea salt
- 1/3 cup coconut sugar
- 1/2 tsp cinnamon
- 1 egg
- 3 Tbsp coconut oil, melted
- 1/2 tsp vanilla extract

Method

1. In a large mixing bowl, stir together almond meal, coconut, chocolate chips/cacao nibs, baking powder, cinnamon, salt and coconut sugar.
2. In a separate bowl, beat egg until uniform in color and doubled in volume.
3. Whisk in the coconut oil and vanilla, then add to dry ingredients and mix until just combined.
4. Chill in the fridge for at least 30 minutes or overnight.
5. Preheat oven to 375F degrees.
6. Shape dough into 1-inch balls, place on baking sheet with 1-1/2 inch space in between each. Press down slightly to flatten a bit.
7. Bake until edges begin to brown, 7-10 minutes.
8. Remove from oven and let cool before serving.
9. Makes approximately 12-15 cookies.

Share your creations with #JLWCookbook | Recipe by: Jesse Lane Lee

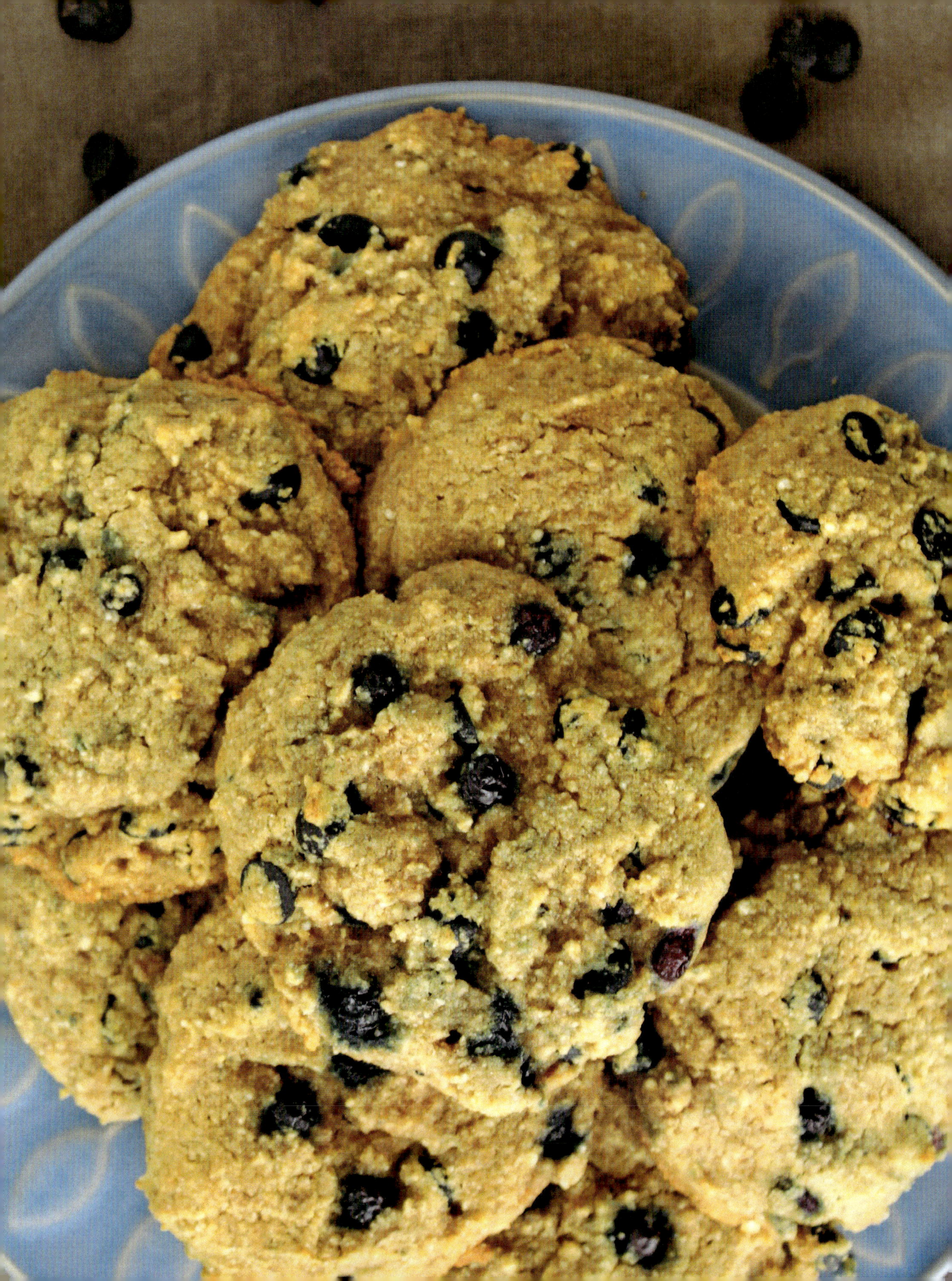

Gluten Free Blueberry Cookies

NF V GF

Prep time: 10 minutes | Cooking time: 20 minutes | Serving Size: 15

I have to admit, cookies are something I miss the most after cleaning up my diet. Delicious gluten free cookies are few and far between, and the cookies that are tasty tend to be laden with dairy, refined sugars and who knows what else. So, even if they taste good, the repercussions of eating them (bloating, acne, upset tummy) just aren't worth it. You can imagine my excitement when I came across a recipe that was free of gunk and ACTUALLY tasted good. Good enough to bring to a party for people who eat 'normally'.

Ingredients

Wet

- 3/4 cup apple sauce
- 1/4 cup maple syrup
- 2 tsp vanilla
- 1/3 cup coconut oil (melted)

Dry

- 1 cup brown rice flour
- 1/2 cup quinoa flour (option to sub GF oats)
- 1 tsp baking soda
- 1 cup blueberries (or half chocolate chips and half blueberries)
- pinch of sea salt

Method

1. Preheat oven to 300F
2. Begin to melt coconut oil on the stove.
3. Mix flours and baking soda in a bowl.
4. Mix all wet ingredients, except coconut oil, in another bowl.
5. Mix wet and dry ingredients together.
6. Stir in chocolate chips and blueberries, gently.
7. Slowly mix in coconut oil to batter until it's fully mixed.
8. Place 1-2 Tbsp of batter on cookie sheet lined with parchment paper.
9. Bake for 18-20 minutes

Share your creations with #JLWCookbook | Recipe by: Mandy King

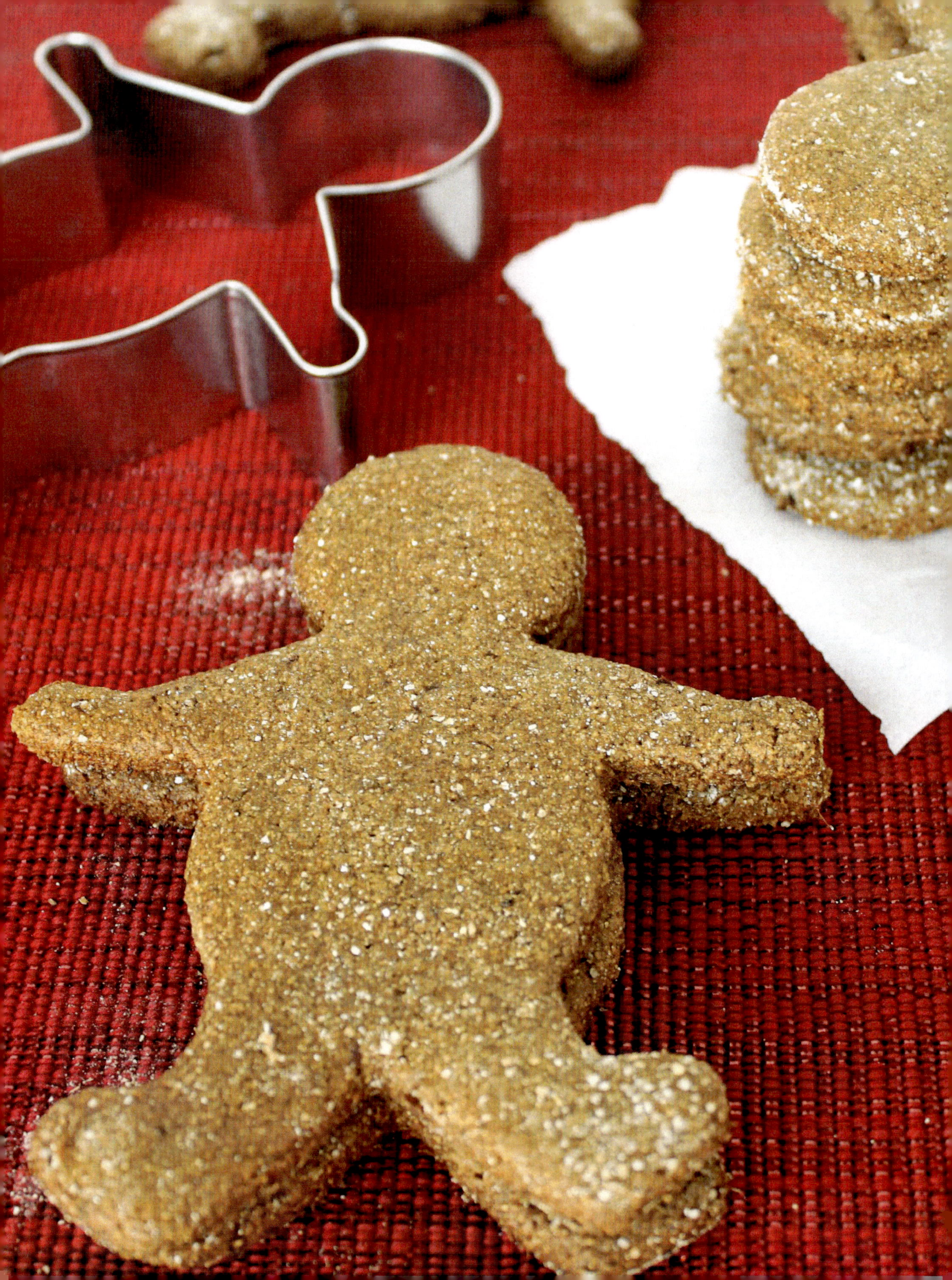

Real Food Gingerbread

NF

Prep time: 15 mins | Inactive time 3 hrs | Cooking time: 12 mins | Serving Size: 16-27 cookies

It took a couple of trials for me to perfect these Gingerbread Men. I wanted to develop a cookie that doesn't contain boatloads of sugar, is limited in processed ingredients and actually has some nutrients (bonus!). All while remaining a "treat" and a respectable Gingerbread Man that is unrecognizable as a "healthy alternative". I think I achieved all of this with this recipe.

Ingredients

- 3 1/2 Tbsp coconut oil
- 3/4 cup date paste, roughly 12 medjool dates blended into a paste
- 1/2 cup coconut palm sugar
- 1 egg
- 1 Tbsp fresh grated ginger (optional)
- 1/3 cup organic blackstrap molasses (not regular molasses)
- 3 cups spelt flour (plus extra for dusting)
- 1 tsp baking soda
- 2 tsp ground ginger
- 1 tsp cinnamon
- 1/2 tsp all spice
- 1/2 tsp ground cloves

Method

1. Put the first 5 ingredients into a large bowl (or stand mixer) and beat until well combined.
2. Add molasses and mix well.
3. In a separate bowl, combine remaining dry ingredients.
4. Add dry ingredients to wet ingredients and stir together until well mixed.
5. The dough mixture is going to VERY sticky at this point. Don't panic. Do your best to scrape as much of it from the bowl and divide it into two flat balls.
6. Put the balls back into the bowl, cover with saran wrap and put back in the fridge. Let it chill for 2-3 hours.
7. Preheat oven to 350F and cover your work surface with a generous amount of spelt flour.
8. Remove one of the dough balls from the fridge and roll it out with a rolling-pin to about 1/4 or 1/8 thickness (if you make them too thin, the cookies will be crispy instead of soft so be careful). If the mixture is sticking, you can roll it out between two sheets of parchment paper.
9. Cut with cookie cutter of your choice or use the rim of a cup and place onto a baking sheet.
10. Roll remaining dough into a ball and put back in the fridge. Repeat above steps with other ball of dough from the fridge, and keep alternating until all the dough is gone.
11. Bake for 10-12 minutes (depending on the heat of your oven).

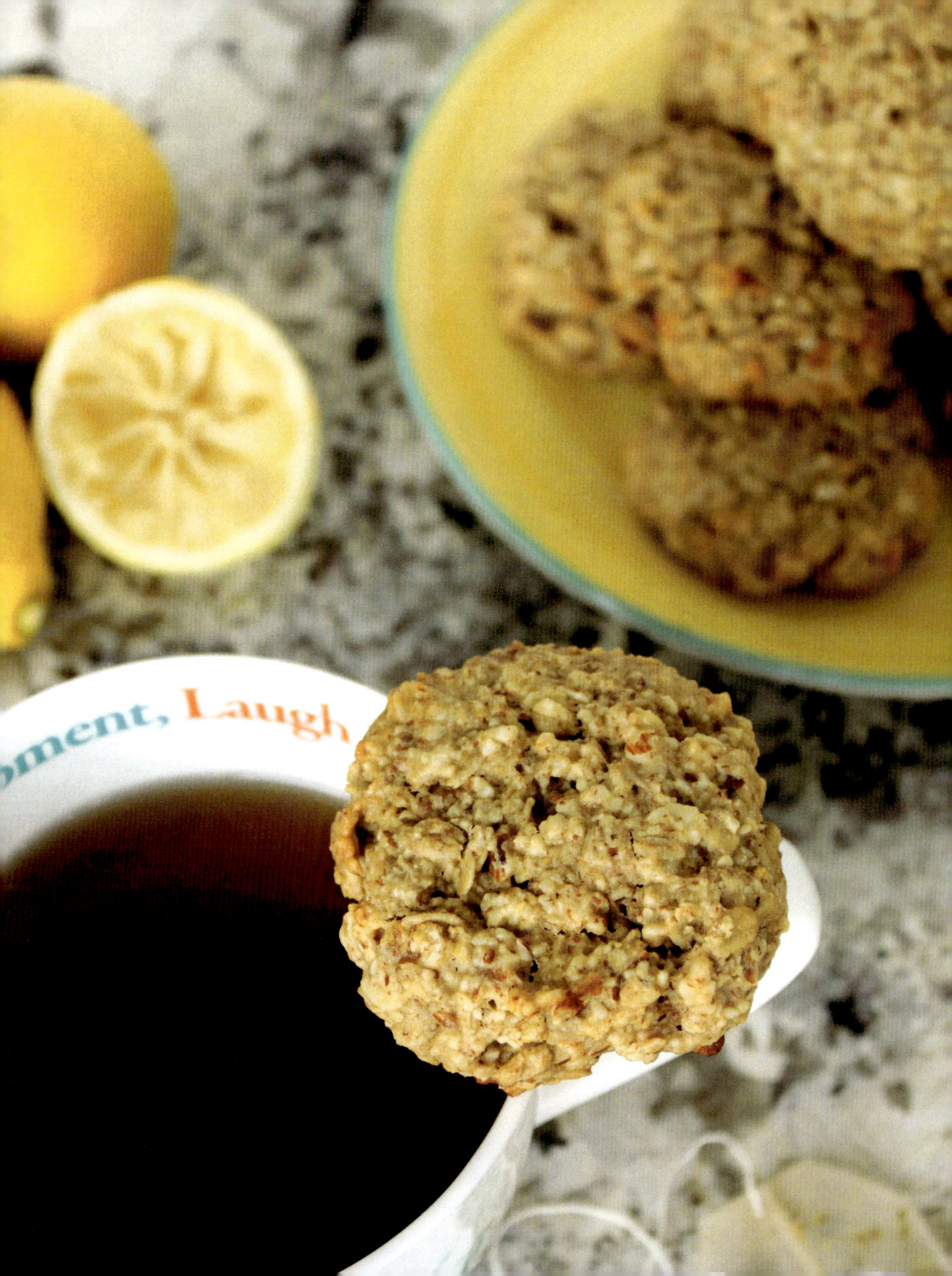
oment, Laugh

Lemon Oatmeal Cookies

GF

Prep: 15 minutes | Cook time: 20 minutes | Serving size: 9

Growing up my Grammy was known for her amazing cookies! Whenever we visited she would always have a bunch of cookie tins packed with cookies in the freezer. Before dinner (or when no one was looking...) we would open them all up and decide which cookies we wanted for dessert. One of my favourite cookies she made was oatmeal lemon, so I decided it was time to create my own healthier version. This recipe is also a great way to use up pulp leftover from making almond milk!

Ingredients

- 1 cup almond pulp* (or use 1 cup of almond meal)
- 1 1/2 cups oats
- 1/3 cup coconut oil, melted
- 1 scoop protein powder, 21g (I use vanilla Sunwarrior)
- 1/4 cup honey
- 1 egg
- 3 Tbsp lemon juice
- Zest of one lemon
- 1 tsp vanilla
- 1/4 tsp baking soda
- 1/4 tsp salt

Method

1. Preheat the oven to 350F and line a baking sheet with parchment paper.
2. Mix all ingredients in a large bowl.
3. Form cookies into 2 Tbsp balls and place on the baking sheet. Bake until golden on the bottom, for 20 minute if you prefer cookie balls and 12 minutes if you flatten them.

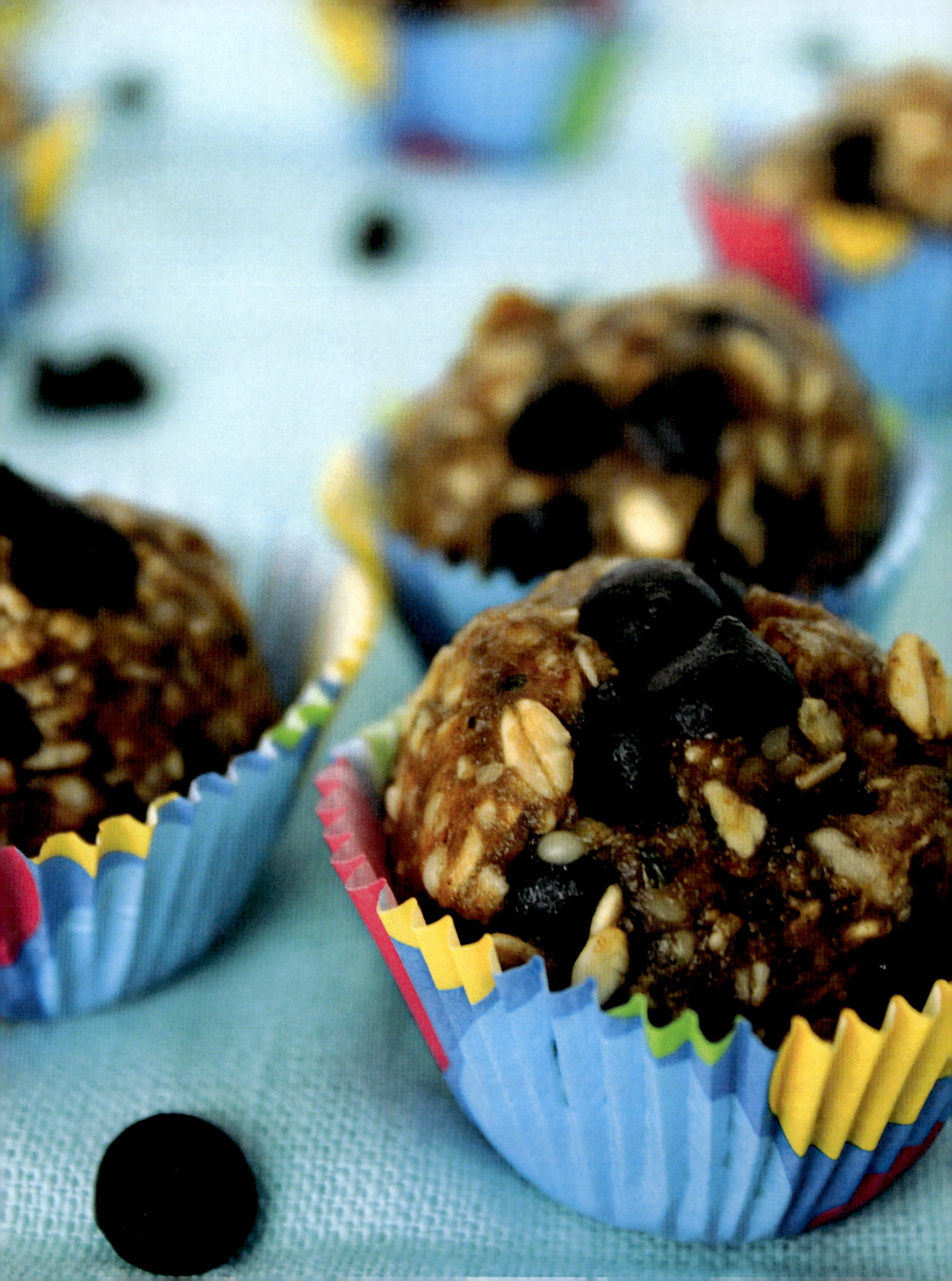

Oatmeal Cookie Truffles

V | NF | GF

Prep time: 20 minutes | Chill time: 2 hours | Serving size: 24 balls

Oatmeal Cookie Truffles are a great excuse to eat cookie dough. I like to make a big batch and store them in the freezer. When I have a craving for something sweet they are ready to enjoy and don't need to be thawed.

Ingredients

- 2 Tbsp ground chia seeds
- 6 Tbsp warm water
- 14 fresh medjool dates, pitted
- 1/2 cup sunflower seed butter
- 4 Tbsp coconut oil
- 2 Tbsp maple syrup
- 2 tsp vanilla extract
- 2 cups gluten-free rolled oats
- 1/3 cup quinoa flakes
- 3 Tbsp hemp seeds
- 1 tsp cinnamon
- 1/3 cup coconut flakes
- 1/4 - 1/3 cup dark chocolate chips or cacao nibs

Method

1. In a small bowl make your chia eggs. Combine 2 Tbsp ground chia seeds with 6 Tbsp warm water and whisk. Let stand for 5 minutes to form a gel like consistency.
2. Place dates into a food processor and pulse until smooth. If your dates are dry, soak them in warm water for 15 minutes to rehydrate them and discard liquid.
3. Add sunflower seed butter, coconut oil, and maple syrup to a saucepan and heat over low heat until melted and combined. Remove from heat, add vanilla and mix well. Pour mixture into food processor with dates and pulse until well combined.
4. Add all dry ingredients, except chocolate chips, to the food possessor followed by chia eggs. Pulse until ingredients are well combined. The dough should hold together and feel slightly sticky.
5. Let mixture cool slightly and add chocolate chips or cacao nibs. If you add the chocolate chips too soon they will melt.
6. Roll into ½ inch balls and place them on a baking sheet lined with parchment paper. Place in freezer for a minimum of 2 hours to set.
7. Once set, store in an airtight container in the fridge or freezer.

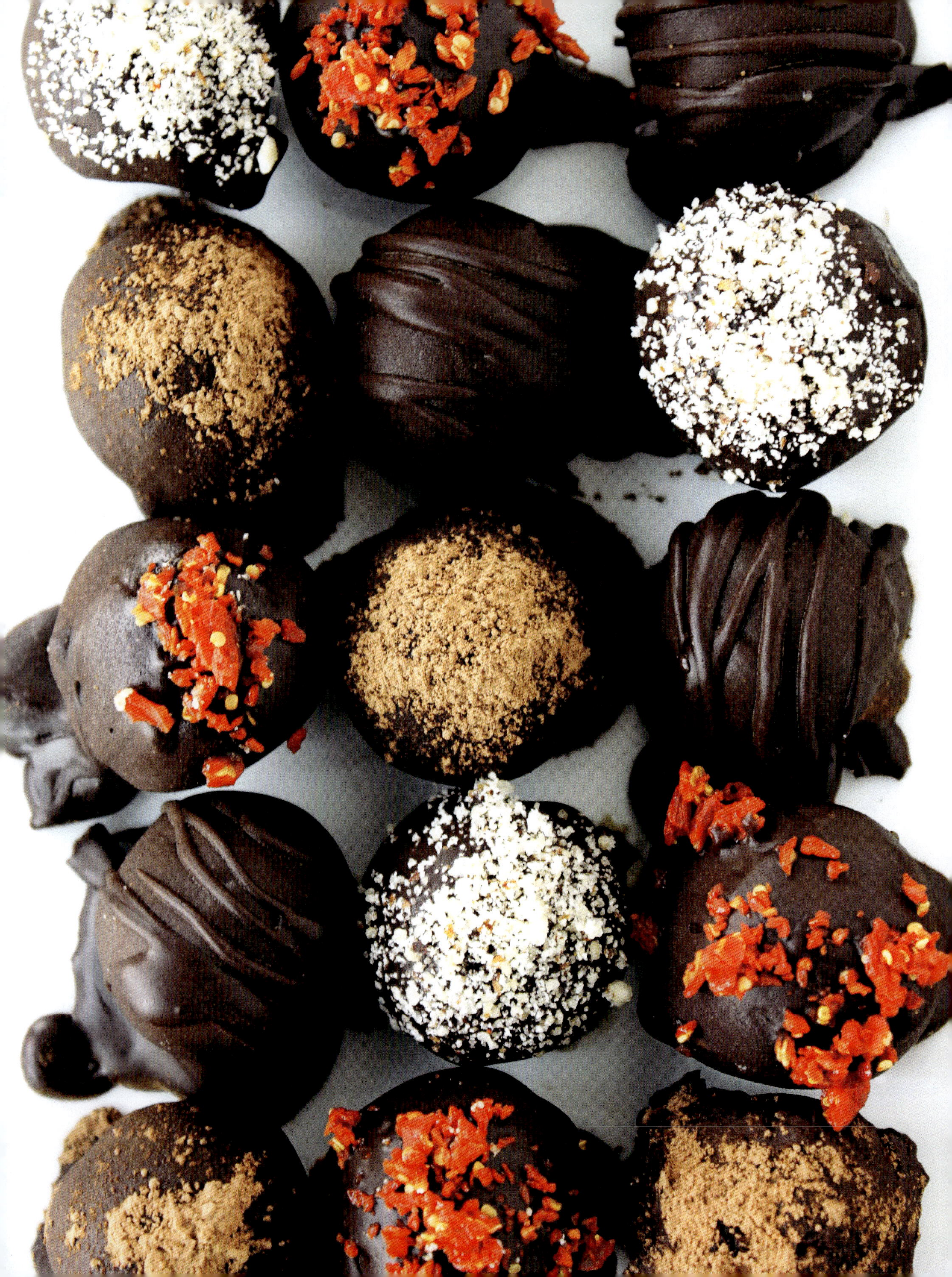

Chocolate Hazelnut Truffles

V | GF

Prep time: 25 minutes | Inactive prep time: 2 hours | Serving size: 15-18 small truffles

Chocolate Hazelnut Truffles are a decadent dessert with a creamy hazelnut center uncased in a dark chocolate shell. These delicious truffles are super easy to make but look fancy. The dark chocolate shell is sweetened with maple syrup and the creamy hazelnut center is sweetened with stevia.

Ingredients

Dark Chocolate Shell
- 1 cup and 1 Tbsp raw cacao powder, sifted if lumpy
- 3/4 cup coconut oil
- 1/4 cup maple syrup
- 1 Tbsp cup goji berries, processed or finely chopped for garnish

Filling
- 1 1/2 cups hazelnuts
- 1/4 tsp stevia
- 1/2 tsp nutritional yeast *optional
- 1 tsp vanilla
- Pinch sea salt

Method

1. Place hazelnuts in a food processor and grind until they becomes a mealy flour. Remove 1 Tbsp of hazelnut flour from the food processor to use as garnish.
2. Add stevia, nutritional yeast, vanilla and salt to the food processor the grind for about 5 to 10 minutes, scraping down the sides as necessary. Keep grinding until the mixture becomes a paste that sticks together when you scrape down the sides. Side note: If you want to make a yummy hazelnut butter keep processing!
3. Form the mixture into 1 Tbsp sized truffles and freeze for 30 minutes.
4. While the truffles are freezing, make the dark chocolate shell by mixing 1 cup raw cacao with melted coconut oil and maple syrup. This mixture should be thick and drippy. If it is too thick place it in a pot over low heat to loosen it up, if it is too thin add additional cacao powder.
5. Once the truffles have hardened, dip them in the chocolate and put them back in the freezer for 10 minutes.
6. Dip the truffles in the chocolate mixture once more and sprinkle with ground hazelnuts, a dusting of raw cacao powder or goji berry pieces immediately. Place in the freezer to set for 1.5 hours.
7. Before serving, thaw at room temperature for 20 minutes or in the fridge for 2 hours.

Share your creations with #JLWCookbook | Recipe by: Jesse Lane Lee

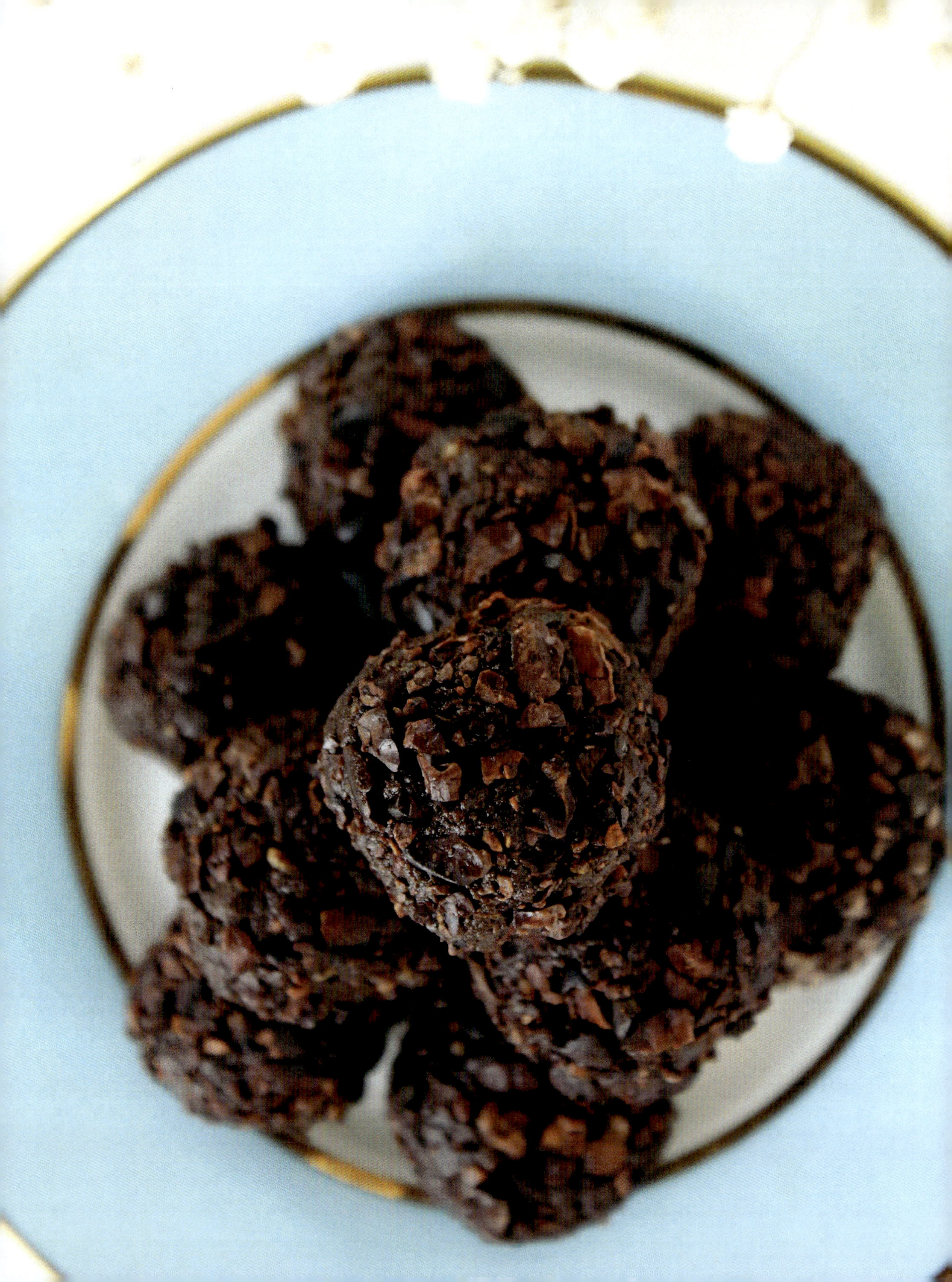

Superfood Choco Truffles

V R SF P GF

Prep time: 15 minutes | Inactive prep time: 30 minutes | Serving size: 18

This is my favorite truffle recipe because it's very simple to make and very tasty. I am always on the go and sometimes I simply don't have the time to prepare a snack before I rush to yoga, spin or an impromptu hike. These little truffles make for a perfect quick and energy filled snack. I have adapted this recipe with two new ingredients for a fresh new taste. The cacao nib coating adds an extra layer of antioxidant power and a little crunch. I adopted this cacao nib idea from my last trip to Hong Kong where I enjoyed a cacao nib truffle at my favorite organic café.

Ingredients

- 1 cup chopped medjool dates
- 1/2 cup chopped walnuts
- 1/3 cup goji berries
- 1/2 cup raw cacao powder
- Zest of 1 lemon or small orange
- 1/3 cup coconut oil, melted
- 1 cup of raw cacao nibs for coating the truffles
- Pinch salt * optional

Method

1. Place the dates and walnuts in a high-speed blender or food processor and pulse until well processed, then add the rest of the ingredients leaving the oil for last. Blend until the mixture clumps together and looks glossy.
2. Remove from the blender and with your clean hands form into balls (size of a walnut) then roll the newly formed globe through the cacao nibs.
3. Place on a baking sheet lined with parchment paper in the fridge for 30 minutes to set before serving. If you live in a warmer climate like me, you will need to keep them in the fridge to avoid melting.
4. Enjoy, 2 to 3 a day, they make a great pre an post workout treat!

Share your creations with #JLWCookbook | Recipe by: Andra Trambitas

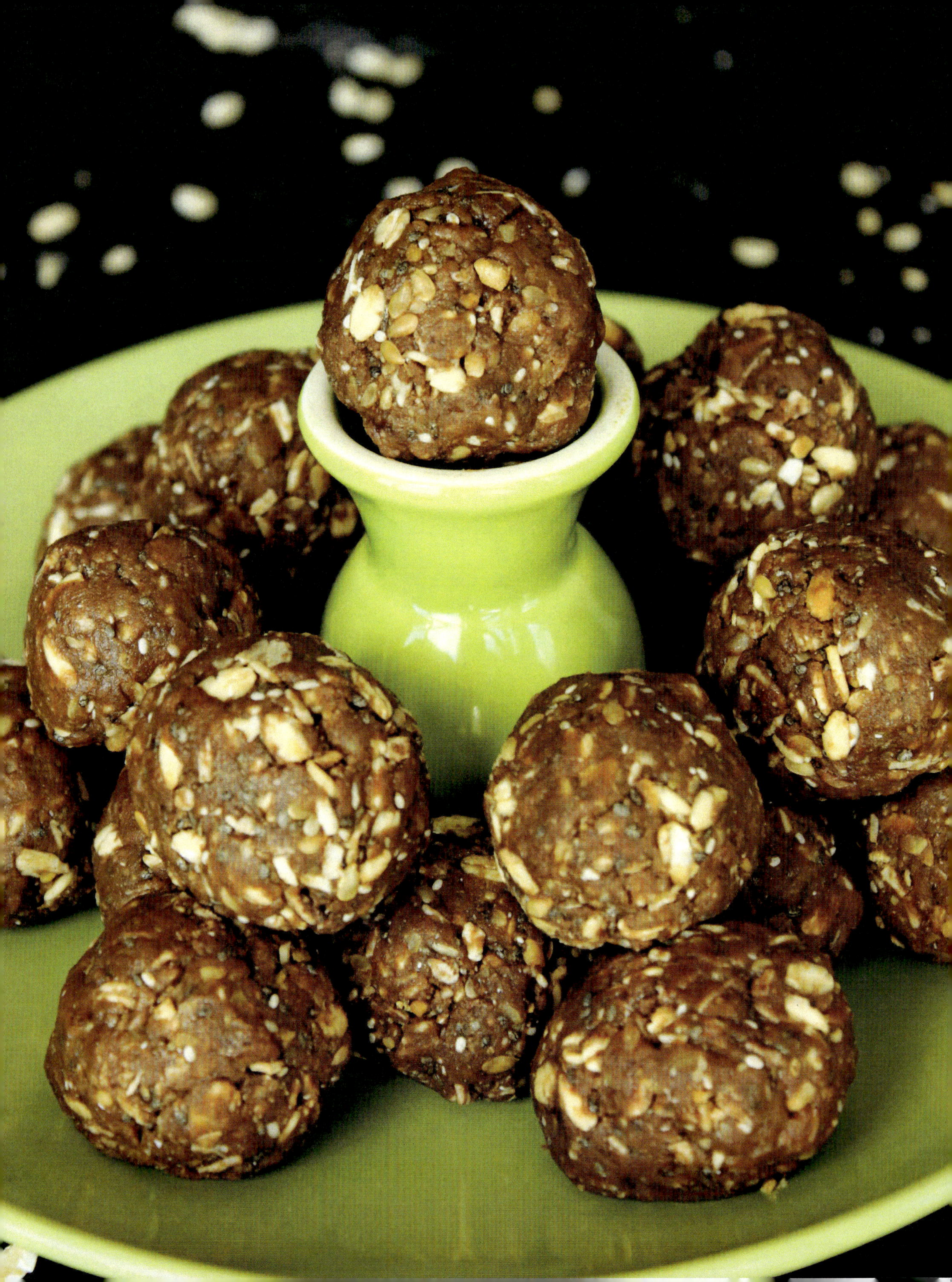

Protein Power Balls

R | GF

Prep time: 15 minutes | Serving size: 24 small balls

Protein Powers Balls are super quick and easy to make. The flavours work so well together creating a delicious dessert that is healthy enough to be a snack. I served these to my non health conscious friends and they couldn't get enough of them!

Ingredients

- 1 cup of gluten free oats
- 2/3 cup of protein powder (your choice of flavour)
- 1/4 cup ground flax seeds
- 1/4 cup chia seeds
- 3 Tbsp unsweetened raw cocoa powder
- 2 Tbsp maca powder
- 3/4 cup almond butter
- 1/3 cup honey
- 1/4 melted coconut oil
- 1 tsp vanilla extract (more to taste)
- 1/4 cup unsweetened shredded coconut

Method

1. Combine all ingredients in a bowl and mix well. If too dry, add a bit more melted coconut oil.
2. Roll into balls.
3. Place on parchment paper and place in fridge. (Or freezer if you enjoy them a little harder and colder)

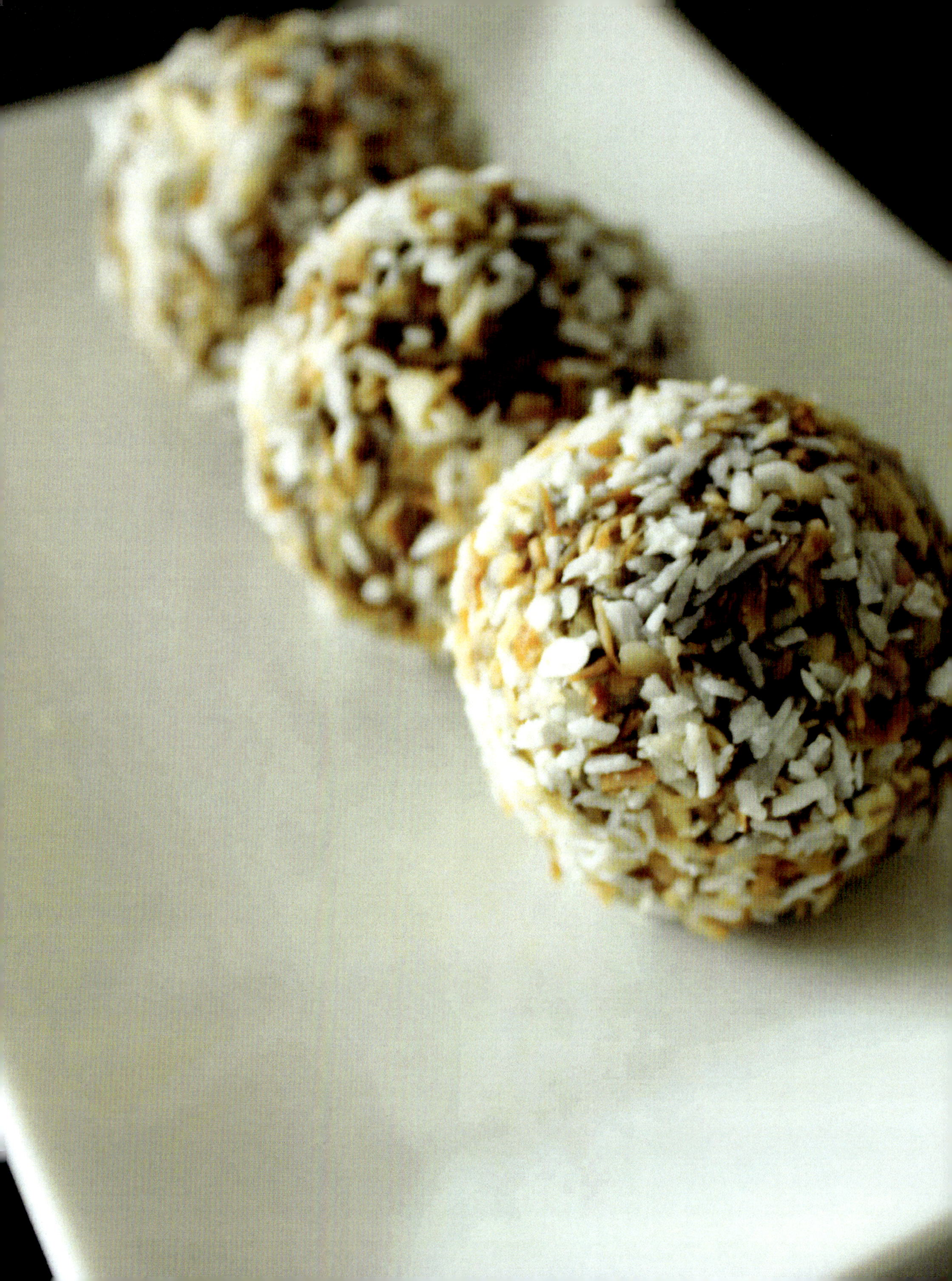

Date Bliss Balls

V R SF P GF

Prep time: 10 minutes | Optional chill time: 30 minutes | Serving size: 12 large balls

Date Bliss Balls are naturally sweetened with dates and full of delicious and nutritious seeds and nuts. They are packed with protein and fibre to give you fuel and the best part is you can make them in less than ten minutes with ingredients that you probably already have in your pantry! Date Bliss Balls are raw so there is no baking required and the nutrients in the ingredients will stay intact.

Ingredients

- 2 cups pitted medjool dates, roughly 20
- 1/4 cup + 2 Tbsp warm water
- 3/4 cup rolled oats
- 1 cup unsweetened coconut flakes
- 1/4 cup raw sesame seeds
- 1/4 cup raw sunflower seeds
- 1/4 cup + 1 Tbsp raw whole almonds, chopped

Method

1. Place dates in the food processor with 2 Tbsp of water and pulse. Slowly add remaining water and process until smooth. If you have a high powered blender you can process the water and dates at the same time without slowly adding the water.
2. Scoop the creamed dates into a bowl and fold in the remaining ingredients, with the exception of ½ cup coconut flakes. If the mixture is soggy then slowly add more oats, if the mixture is too dry slowly add warm water.
3. Shape balls between 3 to 4 cm in diameter and roll them in the reserved ½ cup coconut.
4. Enjoy right away or place on a baking sheet in the freezer for 30 minutes to set. Store in the freezer.

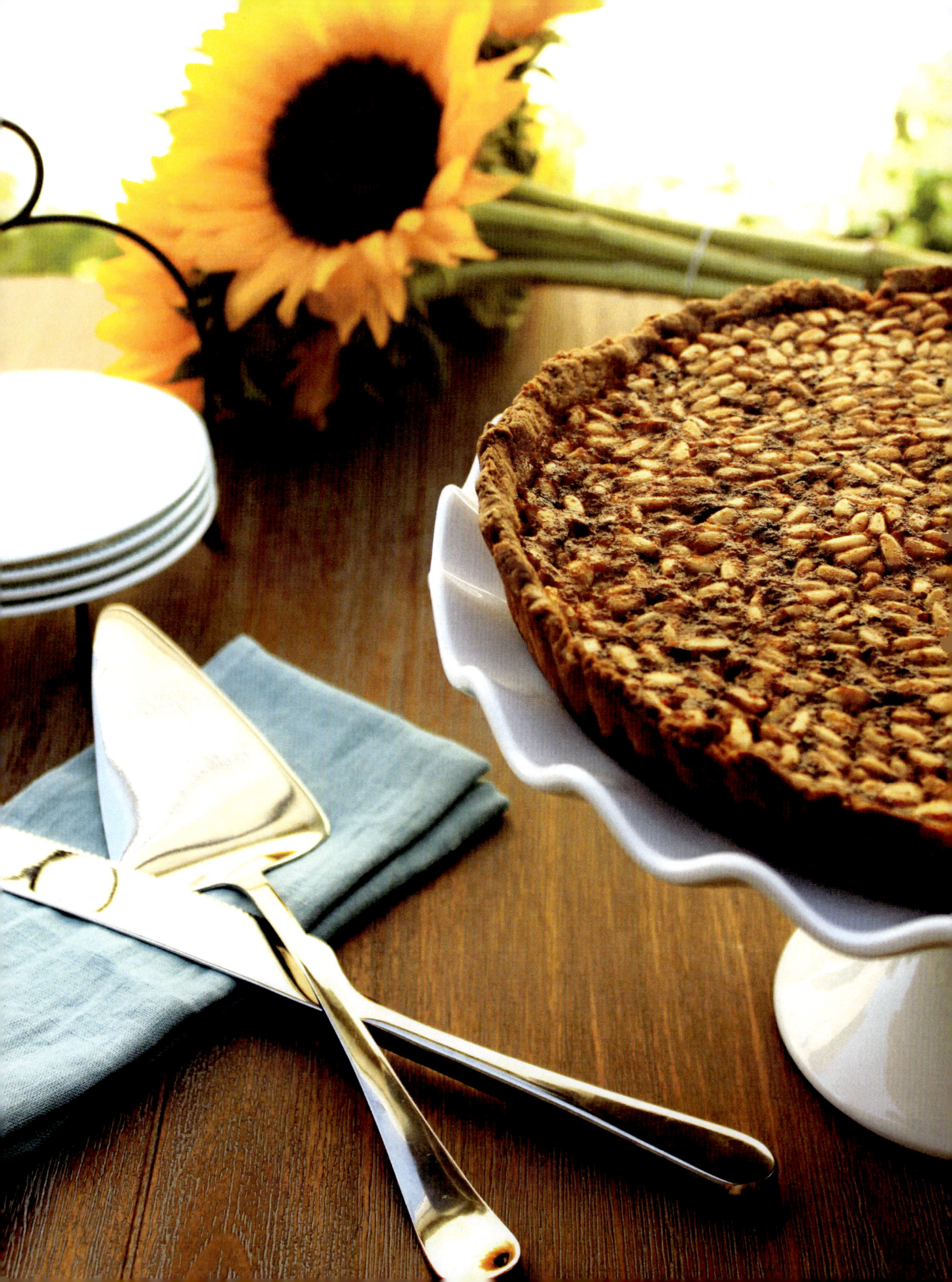

Pine Nut Tart

Prep time: 35 minutes | Inactive prep: 10 minutes | Cook time: 50 minutes | Serving size: 8

This recipe reminds me of the time I lived in the South of France. I just love the creaminess of the pine nuts and the slight sweetness of the honey along with the hint of lemon zest. It's like heaven in your mouth!

Ingredients

Pastry

- 2 cups of spelt flour
- 1/2 cup of chilled coconut oil or butter, cut into cubes
- 2 Tbsp of ground coconut sugar
- 1 egg
- 1-3 Tbsp of iced water
- pinch of salt

Filling

- 1/2 cup of coconut oil
- 1/2 cup of coconut sugar
- 2/3 cup honey or maple syrup
- 3 eggs
- 1 lemon medium, zested and juiced
- Pinch of salt
- 2 cups of pine nuts

Method

1. Preheat the oven to 350F.
2. Sift the spelt flour into a bowl and add to a food processor along with the chilled butter/coconut oil. Pulse until mixture resembles bread crumbs.
3. Add the ground coconut sugar and pulse until mixed.
4. Add the egg and 1 Tbsp of chilled water and mix until the dough is firm, you might have to add a bit more water. Remove from the food processor and form into a ball. Place in a bowl, cover and chill in fridge for about 10 minutes.
5. In the meantime grease, or line your tart tin with parchment paper. Remove dough from the fridge and roll out between 2 pieces of parchment paper, to fit a 9 inch tart tin.
6. Gently place your dough in the pan and press the sides into the pan. Prick holes in the bottom with a fork and place a piece of parchment paper on top. Add baking beads or dried beans and bake for 10 minutes. Take out from the oven and remove the beads/beans and parchment paper.
7. In the meantime, melt your honey or maple syrup over low heat and set aside.
8. Using a hand held mixer, cream together your sugar and coconut oil. Add 1 egg at a time and beat and until well mixed.
9. Stir in your honey or maple syrup, lemon juice and zest, pine nuts, and a pinch of salt.
10. Pour the mixture into your tart pan and bake for 40-45 minutes, until the top is light brown. You may want to put the tart pan on a cookie sheet in case it the filling bubbles over.

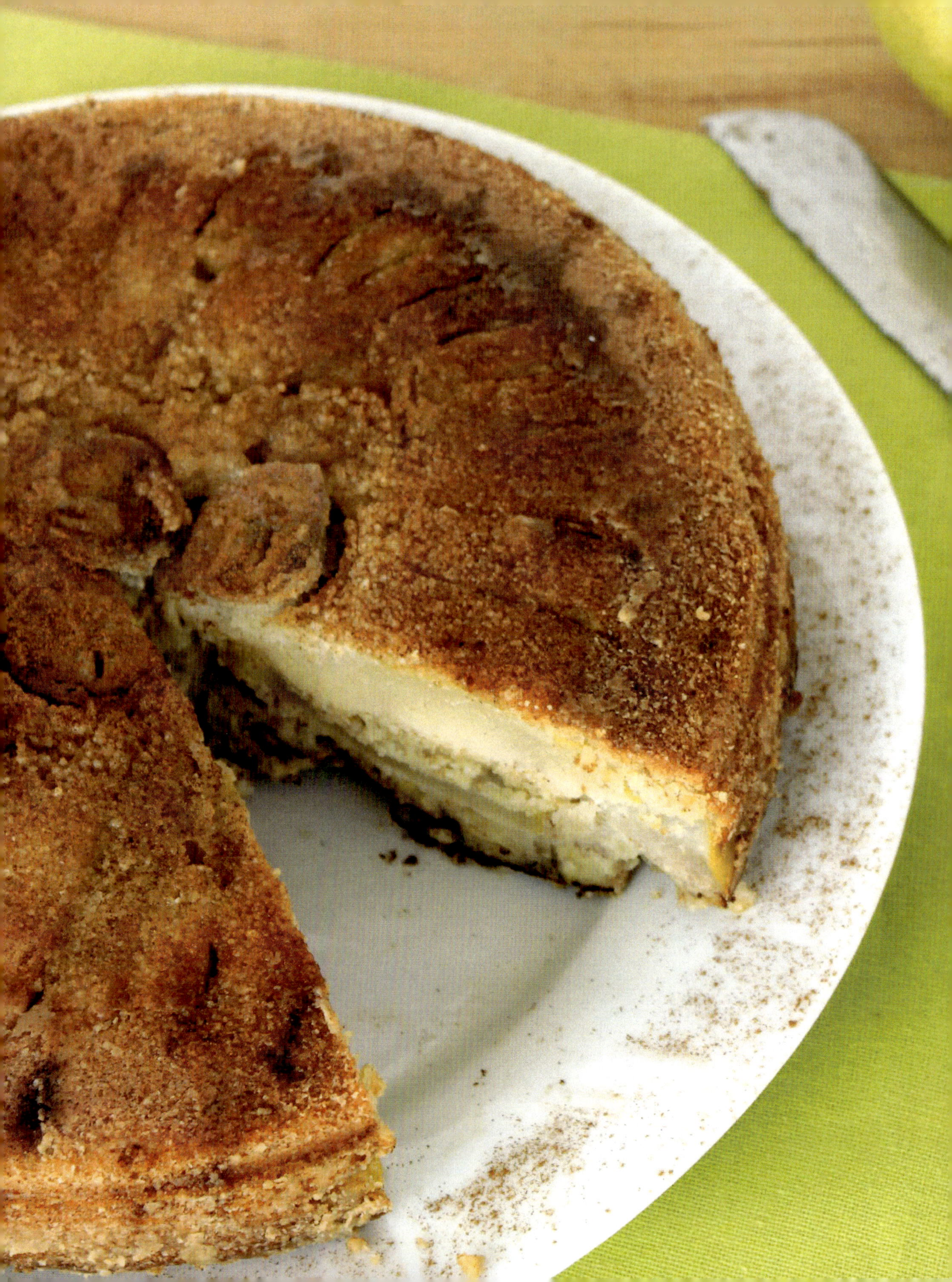

Upside Down Pear-Banana Cake

Prep time: 20 minutes | Cook time: 35 minutes | Serving size: 12

This delicious and easy recipe is free from gluten, dairy, soy as well as processed and refined sugars. This cake is great for entertaining and deceptively easy to make. It is also perfect for people who choose to be vegetarian, suffer from dairy and wheat allergies, or for those who simply love to eat a healthy, wholesome treat.

Ingredients

- 2 Tbsp tahini
- 3 pears
- 2 bananas
- 1/2 cup raw pecans
- 1 Tbsp ground cinnamon
- 1/2 cup + 2 Tbsp maple syrup
- 3 eggs
- 1/2 cup milk alternative
- 1 cup brown rice flour
- 1/2 cup freshly ground flax seed
- 1 tsp baking powder
- Pinch salt

Method

1. Grease 10" round baking pan with tahini and preheat the oven to 375F.
2. Slice pears and arrange them on top of the tahini in the bottom of the pan.
3. Slice bananas and place them onto of the sliced pears.
4. Roughly chop pecans with a knife and sprinkle along with the cinnamon on top of the banana and pear slices. Drizzle 2 Tbsp of maple syrup on top.
5. In a bowl, whisk together the eggs, 1/2 cup of maple syrup and milk alternative and mix thoroughly.
6. In a separate bowl, mix together rice flour, flax meal, baking powder and salt. Combine egg and flour mixture slowly. When incorporated, whisk for 30 seconds.
7. Pour the batter onto of the sliced fruits and chopped nuts.
8. Bake on the middle rack of your oven at 375F for 35 minutes. Pull out of the oven and let cool. Once cooled, flip cake upside down on a serving plate. The sliced fruit will be the top of your cake.
9. Enjoy as is or topped with Banana Protein "Ice Cream"!

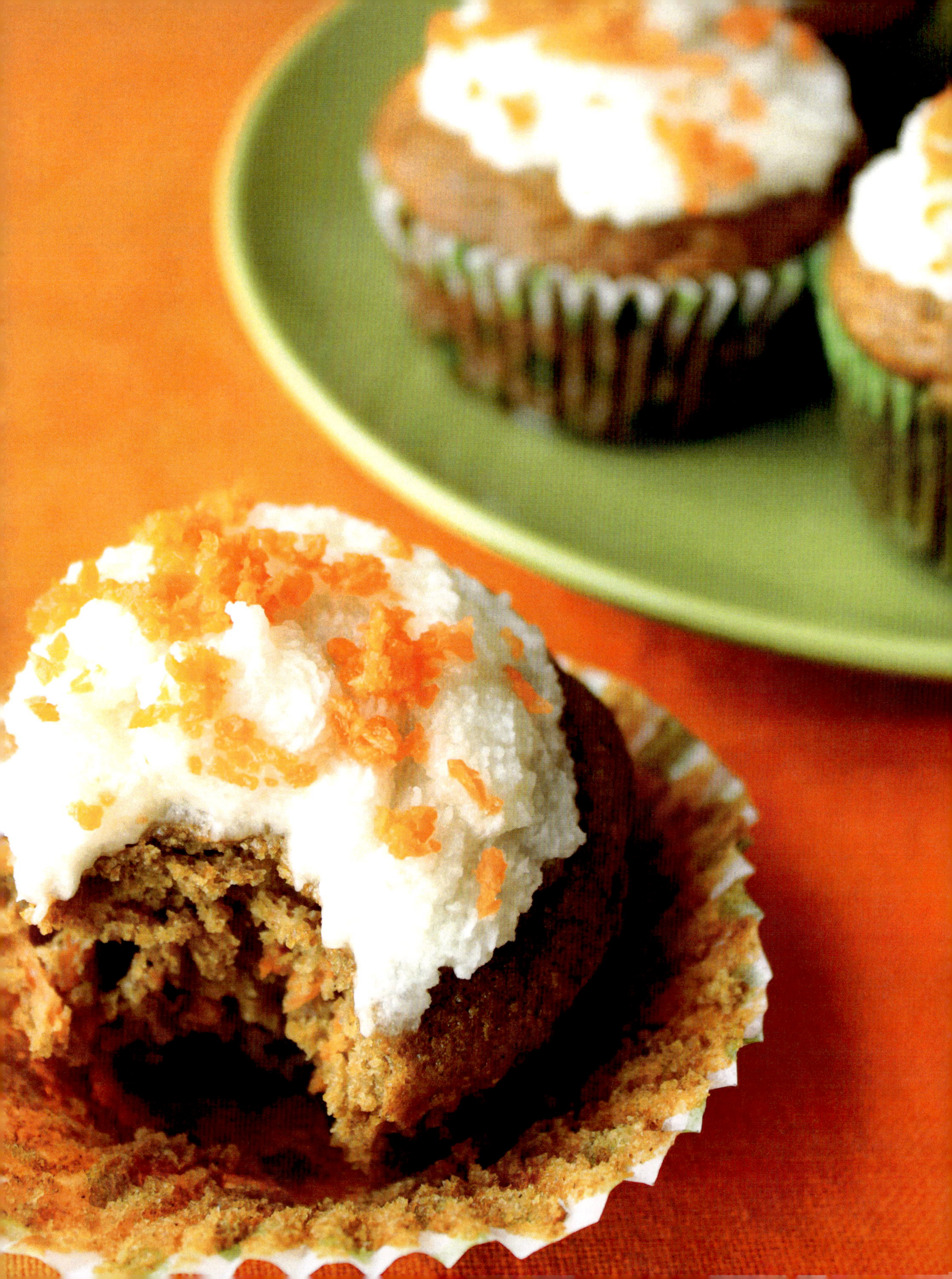

Carrot Cake Cupcakes

NF

Prep time: 5 minutes | Inactive prep time: 2 hours | Serving size: 2

Everyone loves carrot cake but it is so much more fun in cupcake form! These Carrot Cake Cupcakes have the traditional carrot cake flavors; the grated carrots add fiber and make the cupcakes super moist. The coconut cream cheese icing is vegan, but you would never know! I have actually tricked people into thinking it was traditional cream cheese icing. The sprinkles on my Carrot Cake Cupcakes don't contain any dye or chemicals; can you guess what they are?

Ingredients

- 2 cups spelt flour
- 1 cup coconut sugar
- 2 tsp baking powder
- 1/2 tsp baking soda
- 1 tsp ground cinnamon
- 1/4 tsp ground ginger
- 1/4 cup grape seed oil
- 1 cup milk alternative
- 1 tsp vanilla
- 2 large eggs
- 2 cups grated carrot (4 small carrots)

- Coconut Cream Cheese Icing
- 2 cups golden cane sugar
- 1/2 cup coconut oil, at room temperature
- 1 tsp vanilla
- 1/2 tsp Himalayan salt
- 1/2 Tbsp apple cider vinegar
- 1 Tbsp milk alternative, as required
- 1/2 a small carrot

Method

1. Pre-heat oven to 350F and line a muffin pan with extra-large baking cups.
2. Mix all of the dry cupcake ingredients together with a spoon.
3. In a separate bowl, whisk the wet cupcake ingredients together until frothy.
4. Add the wet ingredients to the dry ingredients and stir until mixed, then fold in the grated carrots.
5. Pour the batter into the baking cups, filling them 1-2cm from the top of the baking cup. Cook for 25 minutes or until the tooth pick inserted in the center comes out clean.
6. To make the icing, processed 2 cups of golden cane sugar in a food processor (I used a Magic Bullet).
7. Cream the coconut oil, vanilla, salt and icing sugar together. The coconut oil should be a buttery consistency at room temperature, if it is rock hard you may need to gently soften it.
8. Add the apple cider vinegar and mix. Slowly add the milk until the desired consistency is reached at room temperature. The coconut oil will liquefy at 24C, so to ensure the proper consistency is reached, prepare the filling in the same temperature it will be served in, adjusting the consistency by adding milk or additional icing sugar.
9. Let the Carrot Cake Cupcakes cool for at least 30 minutes, then spread the icing on the cooled cupcakes using a knife or piping bag.

Share your creations with #JLWCookbook | Recipe by: Jesse Lane Lee

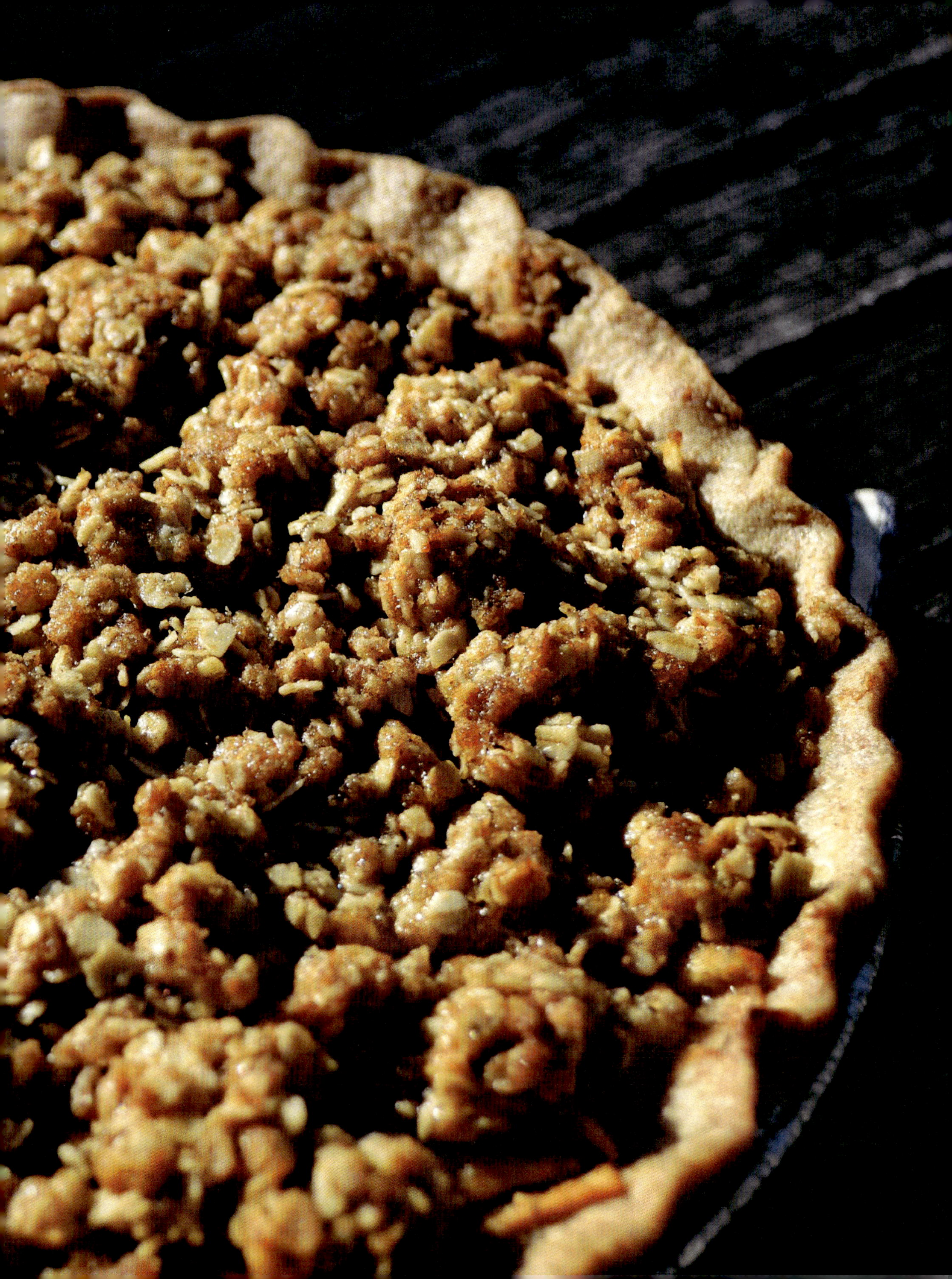

Pear Apple Pie Crumble

Prep time: 30 minutes | Inactive prep time: 1 hour | Cook time: 50 minutes

Pear Apple Pie Crumble is perfect for the fall season and makes a sweet ending to your Thanksgiving feast. It contains seasonal apples and pears nestled in a flaky spelt crust topped with a sweet crumble. I like to use spelt flour in this recipe because it adds a delicious nutty flavor to the crust and it is a great source of manganese, which is important for healthy joints.

Ingredients

Crust

- 1 1/4 cups spelt flour
- 1/4 tsp salt
- 1/4 tsp cinnamon
- 1/4 cup + 2 Tbsp organic butter or coconut oil, chilled and cut into cubes
- 3 to 4 Tbsp cold water

Crumble Topping

- 1/2 cup coconut oil, softened
- 1/2 cup coconut sugar
- 1/2 tsp vanilla

Filling

- 1/3 cup coconut sugar
- 1/4 cup spelt flour
- 1/2 tsp cinnamon
- 1/2 tsp ground nutmeg
- 2 large apples, peeled and sliced
- 1 large pear, peeled and sliced

- 1/3 cup spelt flour
- 1 tsp cinnamon
- 1 cup oats

Method

1. For Crust. Mix flour, salt and cinnamon in a food processor fitted with the metal blade or by hand. Cut chilled butter/coconut oil into chunks and add it to the food processor and process until the butter/coconut oil is the size of peas. If you are mixing by hand, use a pastry blender or two knives to cut the coconut oil into the flour, do not stir.
2. Slowly add cold water until the mixture holds together.
3. Form the pastry into a disk and place in the refrigerator to chill for an hour.
4. While the crust is chilling, mix the sugar, flour, cinnamon, nutmeg and salt in a bowl. Add the apples and pear; toss to coat.
5. Mix all the topping ingredients together a separate bowl and set aside.
6. Preheat oven to 350F and Remove the chilled dough from the fridge and place on a large sheet of parchment paper. Roll out the dough with a floured rolling pin until it is 1/8 inch thick and roughly 12-inches in diameter (for a 9-inch pie plate).
7. Place the rolled out dough on the pie plate and trim the edges leaving an extra half inch. Tuck the extra dough underneath itself to form a thick edge and flute.
8. Add the pear and apple mixture, top with the crumble topping and bake for 50 minutes. Check the pie after 20 minutes and if the crust edges are getting dark cover them with foil. Cover the rest of the pie for the last 10 minutes of cooking if the topping is golden brown.

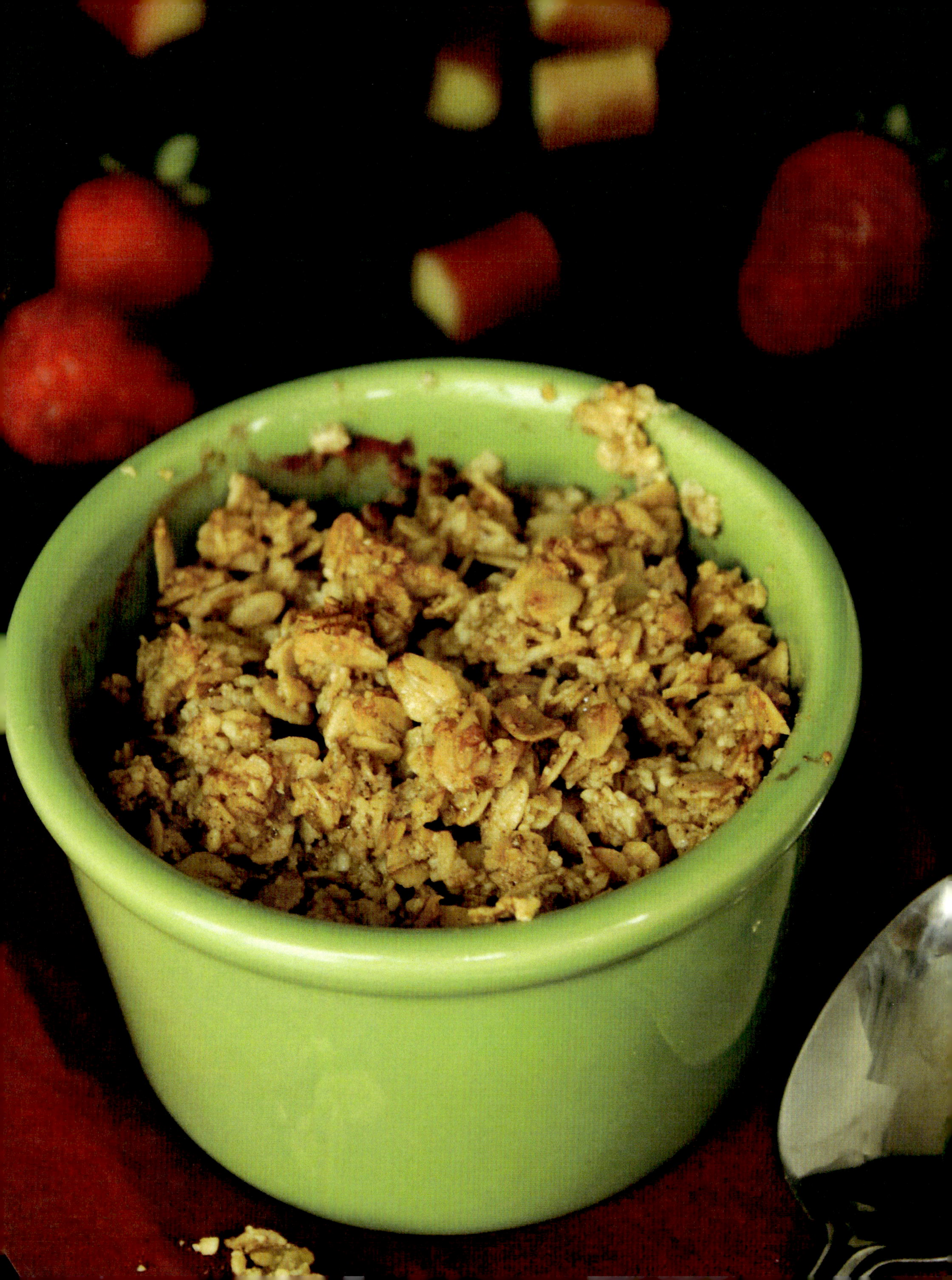

Strawberry Rhubarb Crisp

V GF

Prep time: 10 minutes | Cook time: 30 minutes | Serving size: 4

Strawberry Rhubarb Crisp is one of my favorite quick and easy summer desserts. It is bursting with sweet juicy strawberries and sour rhubarb topped with a golden gluten free crumble. Strawberry Rhubarb Crisp is naturally sweetened with a touch of maple syrup which makes for a refreshing vegan dessert. I have always been a rhubarb lover. My mom grew rhubarb in her garden and the two of us would enjoy it freshly picked dipped in a little sugar. I LOVE the tart sour flavor of rhubarb that pairs so well with strawberries.

Ingredients

Strawberry Rhubarb Filling

- 1/4 cup almond flour
- 2 Tbsp ground chia seeds
- 1/2 lemon, zested and juiced
- 2 Tbsp maple syrup
- 2 cup strawberries, quartered
- 2 cup rhubarb, cut into 2cm slices

Gluten Free Crumble Topping

- 1 cup gluten free oats
- 1/2 cup almond flour
- 1/4 cup coconut oil, softened
- 1/4 cup maple syrup
- 1 tsp cinnamon
- 1/2 tsp vanilla

Method

1. Preheat the oven to 350F. Grease four 1 cup ramekins with coconut oil and place them on a baking sheet.
2. Mix almond flour, ground chia seeds, lemon zest, lemon juice and maple syrup in a bowl. Add strawberries and rhubarb and stir until evenly coated.
3. Mix all the gluten free crumble topping ingredients together in a separate bowl and set aside.
4. Place the strawberry rhubarb crisp filling into four 1 cup ramekins and top with the crumble topping.
5. Bake for 30 minutes until the strawberry rhubarb crisp filling has softened and the juices have released.
6. Remove from the oven and serve with coconut whipped cream, a la mode or as it is.

Share your creations with #JLWCookbook | Recipe by: Jesse Lane Lee

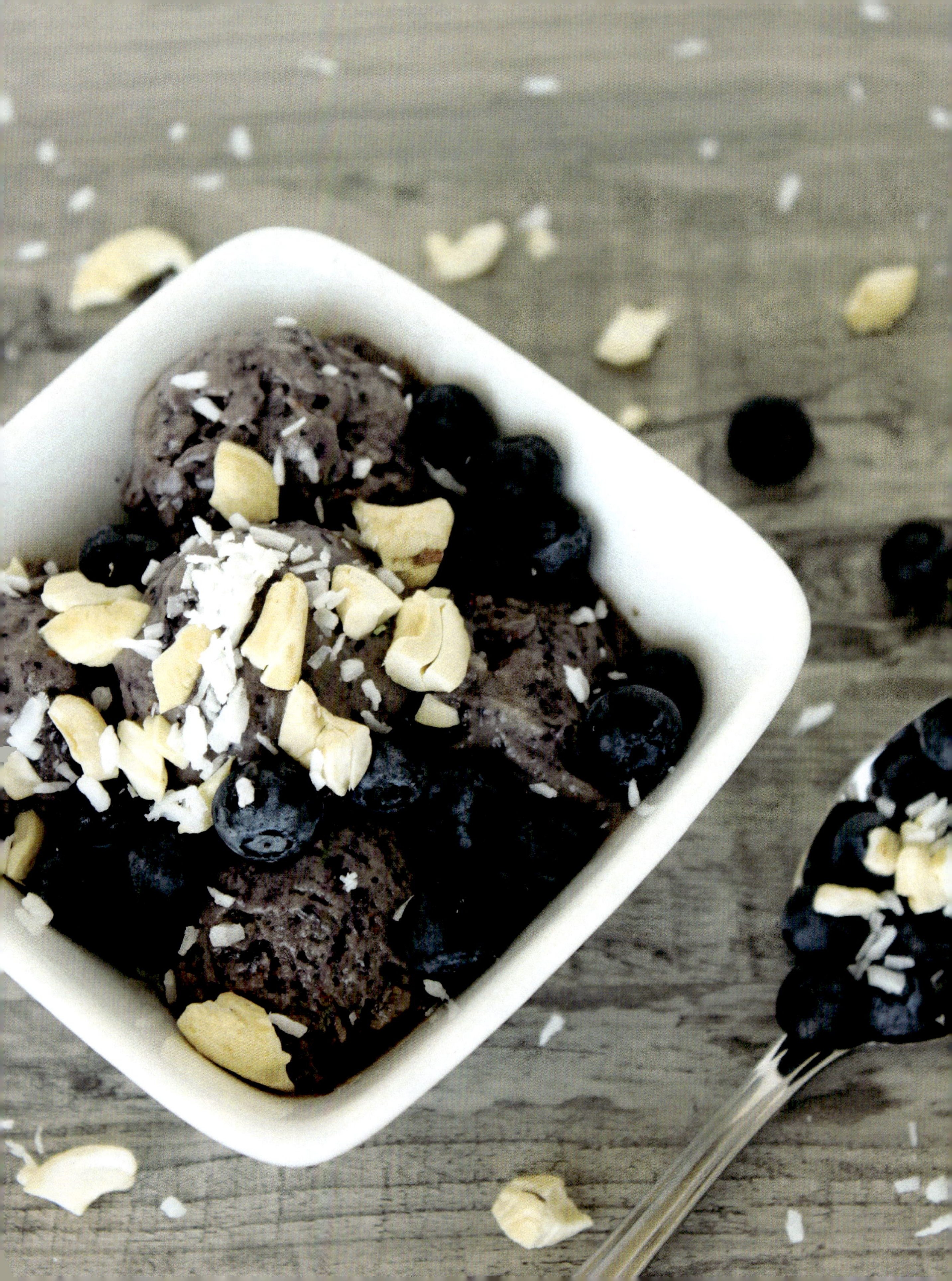

Vegan Blueberry Ice Cream

(V) (R) (SF) (P) (GF)

Prep time: 5 minutes | Inactive prep time: 2 hours | Serving size: 2

I created this recipe because I wanted to enjoy ice cream that is actually healthy! I just love cooling down with ice cream on hot sunny days, but regular ice cream is loaded with dairy, artificial flavoring, thickeners and tons of sugar. Vegan Blueberry Ice Cream is made with whole foods and gets all the sweetness it needs from the banana and blueberries. It is super quick and easy to make and you don't need an ice cream maker!

Ingredients

- 1 frozen banana
- 2 cup blueberries, frozen
- 1/2 tsp minced fresh ginger, or 1/4 tsp ginger powder
- 2 Tbsp cashew butter
- 1-2 Tbsp coconut milk, as required

Method

1. Place the frozen banana, blueberries, ginger and cashew butter, in a food processor and blend until smooth.
2. Add coconut milk slowly until you get an ice cream consistency.
3. Serve immediately.

Blueberries are jam packed with phytonutrients that are both an anti-inflammatory and antioxidant. Antioxidants are essential to neutralizing cancer causing free radicals and reversing the effects of sun damage. Blueberries are excellent for the cardiovascular system because they improve blood fat balances by reducing total cholesterol and supporting healthy blood pressure. Blueberries can actually help regulate blood sugar levels because they have a low glycemic index and are high in fiber.

Share your creations with #JLWCookbook | Recipe by: Jesse Lane Lee

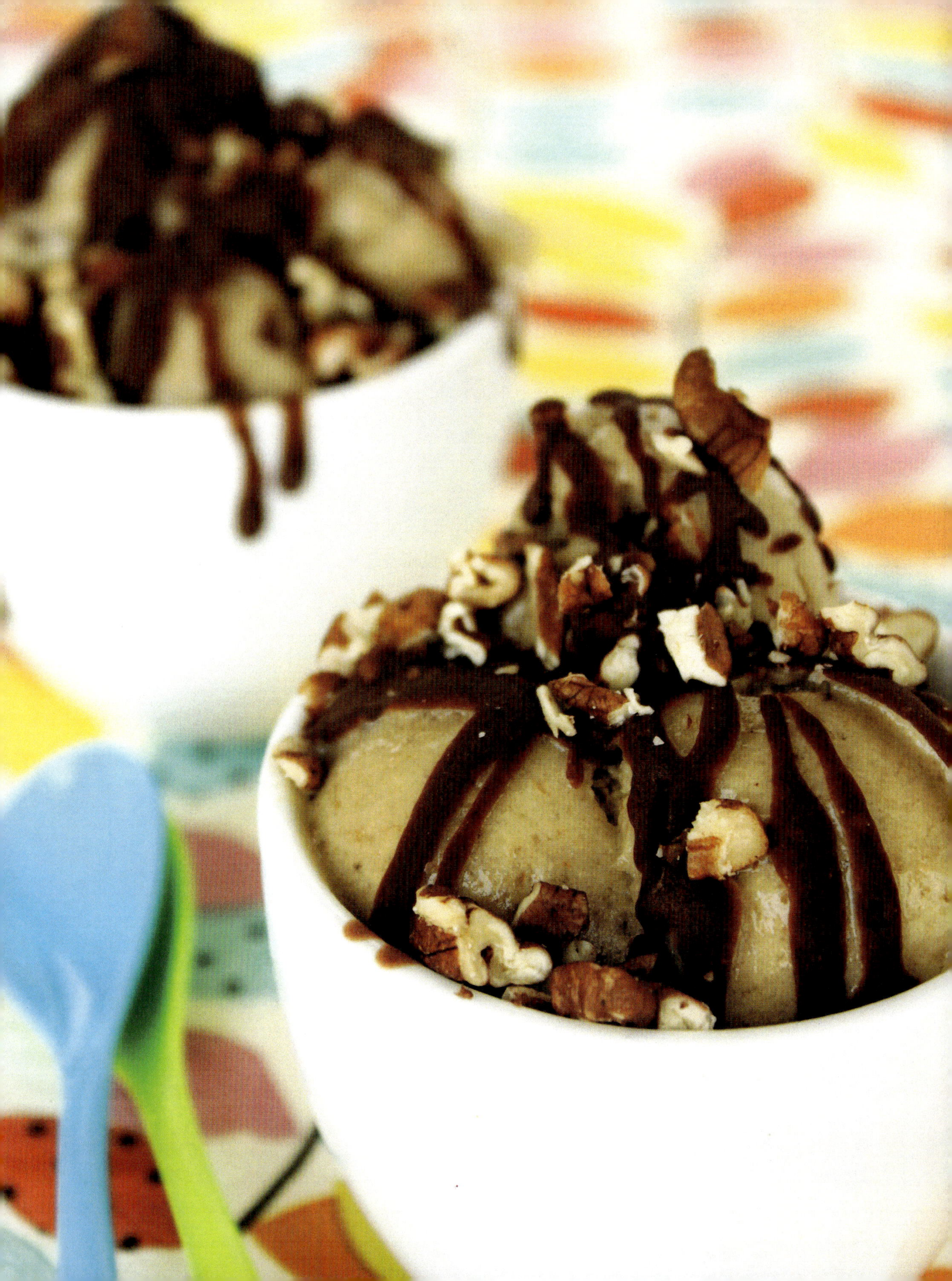

Banana Protein "Ice Cream"

(V) (R) (SF) (P) (GF)

Prep time: 5 minutes | Serving size: 2

You won't believe it's not ice cream! A must try recipe to satisfy a sweet tooth that is totally guilt free!

Ingredients

- 2 bananas frozen in slices
- 1 heaped Tbps vanilla plant based protein powder, or your choice of flavour
- Optional: 5-6 raw cashews (preferably soaked in water for a few hours and drained)

Method

1. Blend in a food processor (note: use a food processer over a blender for a more 'ice cream' like texture). If you wish, you may add a splash of non-dairy milk to help the food processor along; alternatively you can wait a few minutes for the bananas to soften to make blending easier. However, the less liquid you add the more of an ice cream-like texture you achieve. Optional: Garnish with crumbled pecans.

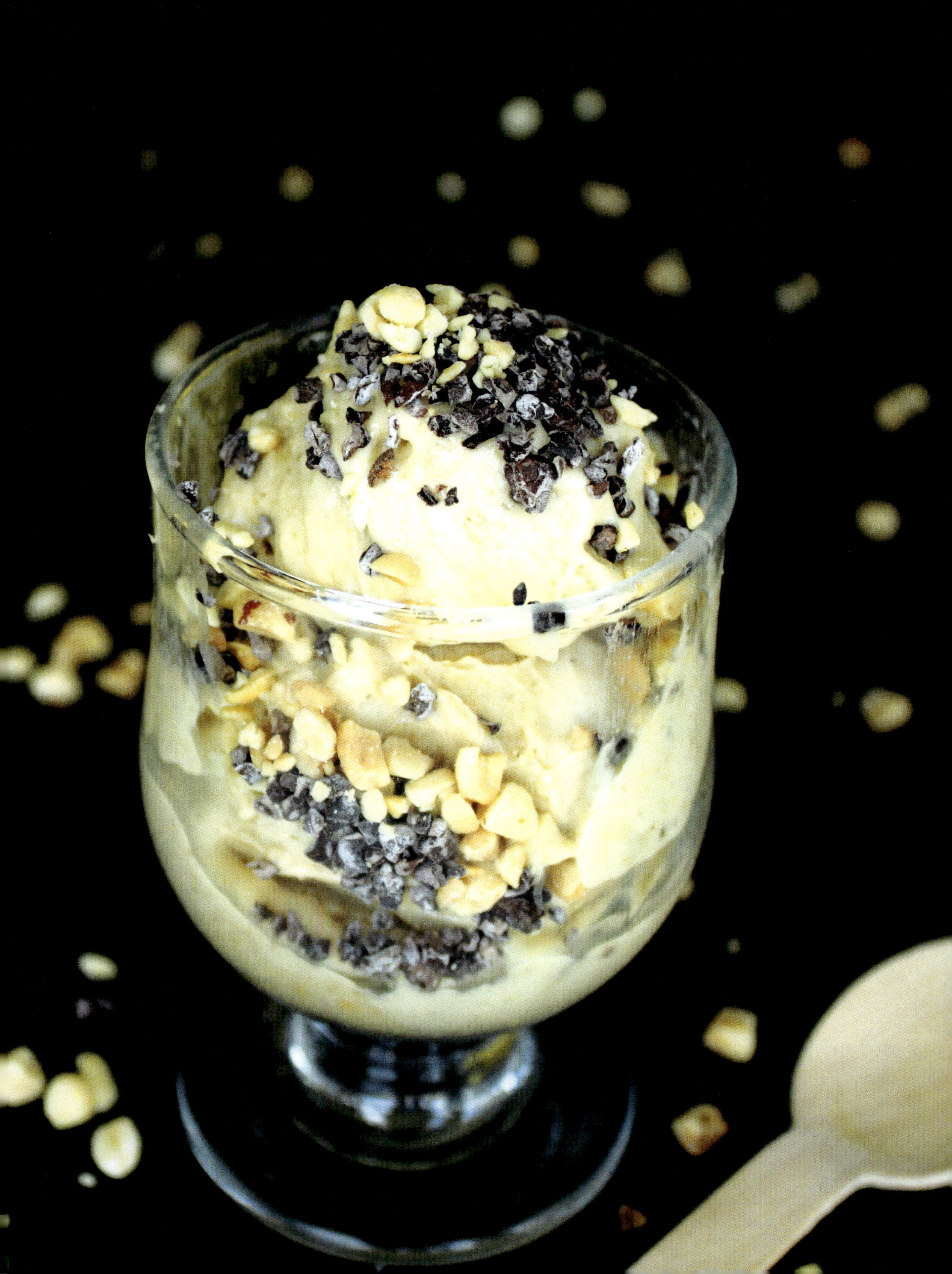

Peanut Butter Soft Serve

V R GF

Prep time: 5 minutes | Serving size: 4

Nothing beats the combination of peanut butter and banana! This ice cream is ready in minutes and is the perfect healthy treat for a hot day. It really does resemble soft serve ice cream. It is great on its own or topped with peanuts and raw cacao nibs.

Ingredients

- 4 bananas, cut into quarters, frozen
- 3 Tbsp natural peanut butter (or any nut butter)
- 1 Tbsp maple syrup

Method

1. Add all ingredients to a food processor and mix until a creamy soft serve constancy is reached.
2. Scoop into a bowl and top with your favourite toppings.

Share your creations with #JLWCookbook | Recipe by: Deanna Harris

Want More?

Holistic IN THE CITY

Free Mini eBook

7 days of smoothies to start your smoothie habit

7 Days of Smoothies

Get my eBook 7 Days of Smoothies for FREE

As a Holistic Nutritionist I drink a lot of smoothies!

Smoothies are a fantastic and easy way to get a big dose of nutrients in the morning.

When I work with busy clients who are looking to clean up their diet, I often recommend they start their day with a smoothie. Smoothies can be made in less than 5 minutes and taken on the go making them super easy to fit into your morning routine.

By signing up for my weekly newsletter you will receive your very own copy of my eBook: 7 Days of Smoothies!

It contains seven holistically delicious smoothie recipes that are made with healthy ingredients and superfoods.

Grab your Copy at: www.jesselanewellness.com/nourish/free-ebook-7-days-smoothies/

Holistic in the City

Tropical Bliss

Ingredients:

1/3 cup frozen mango
1/3 cup fresh pineapple
1/2 frozen banana
2 handfuls of spinach
1 scoop of vanilla protein powder
2 cups almond milk

Serves 1-2

Tropical Bliss smoothie instantly transports you to a tropical paradise just by closing your eyes and taking a sip. The juicy mangoes are concentrated in Vitamin A and the tangy pineapples contain a digestive enzyme called bromelain which is great for reducing bloating.

Holistic IN THE CITY

The Holistic in the City 21 Day Smoothie Guide is perfect for you if you are new to smoothies, or if you are a smoothie veteran who finds themselves in a smoothie rut making the same smoothie every morning. It contains 21 different smoothie recipes made with love by 7 holistic nutritionists. These smoothies make delicious breakfasts or snacks that are bursting with nutrients.

21 Day Smoothie Guide

Want to jump on the smoothie bandwagon but don't know where to start?

Recently smoothies have been all the rage with everyone and their grandma making them in effort improve their health.

The problem is you might be making common smoothie mistakes like forgetting to add protein, fiber and healthy fats and adding way too much fruit and sugary ingredients.

You could be creating a drink that is not only unhealthy but contributing to weight gain!

> "I absolutely LOVED the eBook – a great variety of smoothies with many new ingredients/spices and flavours! I definitely will continue this path of healthy living – enjoying a smoothie every day!"

For less than the price of your morning latte, you can buy The Holistic in the City 21 Day Smoothie Guide!

> "It was a wonderful book with so many good recipes and they were good. Helped me change my morning start from coffee to healthy."

Only $4.99

Grab your Copy at:
http://www.jesselanewellness.com/holistic-city-21-day-smoothie-guide/

Affiliate application

Did you like this eBook and want to share it with your friends and family?

Well now you can AND make a couple dollars on the side. I have an awesome affiliate program where I offer 50% commission!!!

Here's a breakdown of the Jesse Lane Wellness Affiliate Program:

Anyone who has purchased one of my eBooks is welcome to sign up
Your application will be approved if you meet my marketing criteria OR have purchased one of my eBooks
You will earn 50% commission every time someone buys an eBook using your link
Payouts are made quarterly (January, March, June & September) when a minimum of $30 is owed
The Jesse Lane Wellness Affiliate Program applies to product: The Holistic in the City 21 Day Smoothie Guide and Jesse Lane Wellness Cookbook: Healthy Dairy Free Desserts, I will be adding additional eBooks as they are released.

Questions? Send me an email to info@jesselanewellness.com.

To learn more go to www.jesselanewellness.com/affiliate-area/.

Let's get Social

You can connect with me on Facebook or Instagram as @jesselwellness and I'm also on YouTube.

I always get so excited when someone makes one of my recipes and tags me in the picture!!! Use #jlwcookbook and #jlwdairyfreedesserts when you make any of the recipes in the cookbook so I can see and share your beautiful creations.

Website: htpp://www.jesselanewellness.com/

Facebook: @JesseLWellness

Instagram: @JesseLWellness

You Tube: YouTube.com/c/JesseLaneWellnesscom or search Jesse Lane Wellness

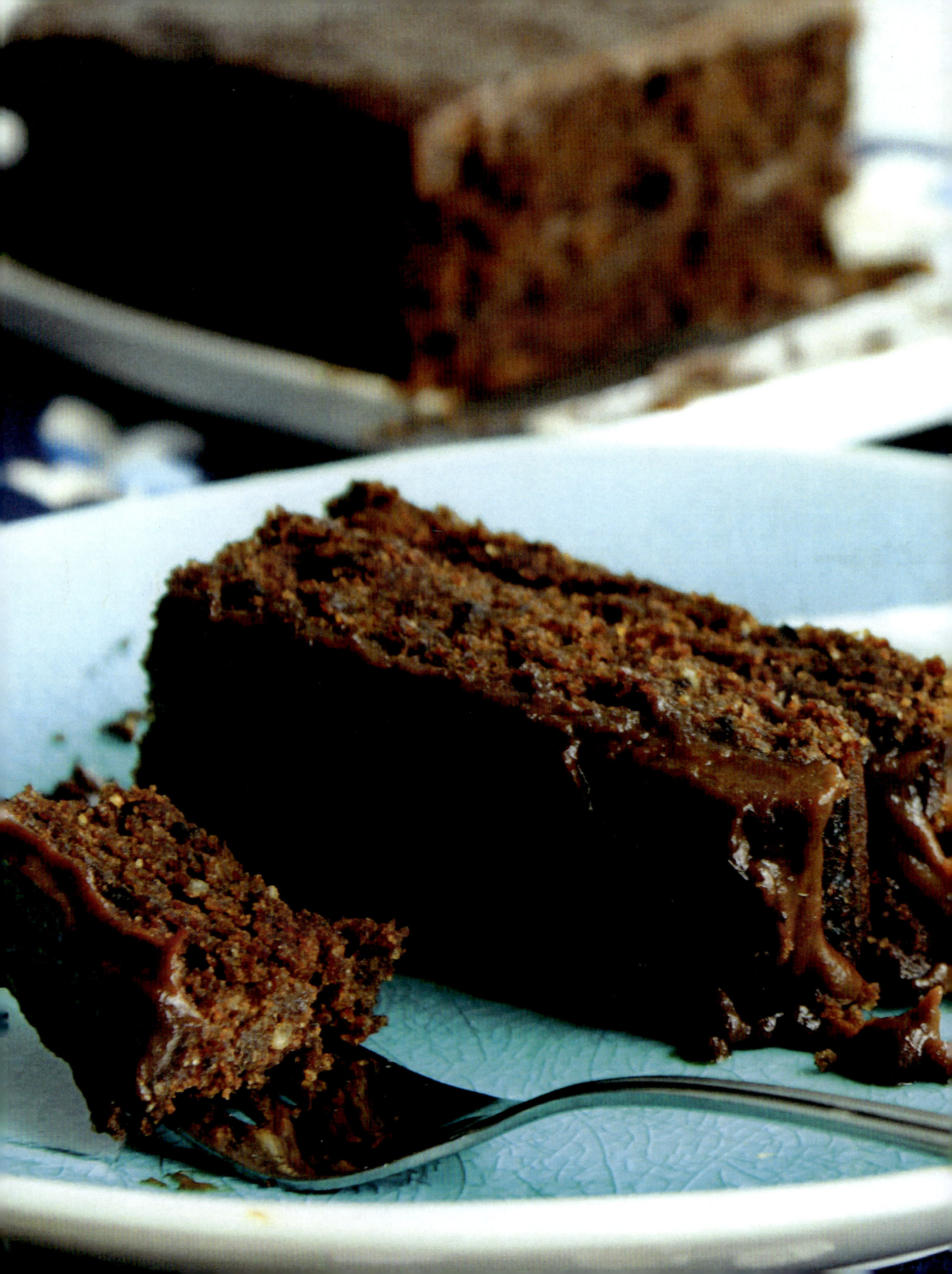

"A party without cake is just a meeting" - Julia Child

Any recommendations in this book are not meant to be considered medical advice; the author is not a doctor. Please discuss your personal health, including any options or ideas you get from this book with your personal, qualified health practitioner before making changes to your diet or adjusting/discontinuing any medication. The author is not responsible for any adverse outcomes associated with using or misconstruing advice or information in this book.

This book is the creative work of Jesse Lane Lee. All information, text and photos are considered copyright of Jesse Lane Wellness and should not be shared, copied or distributed without permission.

Manufactured by Amazon.ca
Acheson, AB